On the Banks of the Wyaloosing

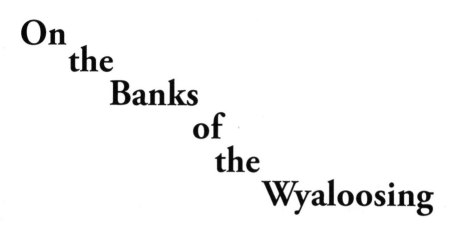

LORALYN REYNOLDS

authorHOUSE®

AuthorHouse™ LLC
1663 Liberty Drive
Bloomington, IN 47403
www.authorhouse.com
Phone: 1-800-839-8640

Published by AuthorHouse   05/13/2014

ISBN: 978-1-4969-0739-4 (sc)
ISBN: 978-1-4969-0738-7 (e)

Library of Congress Control Number: 2014907867

Dedication

Dedicated to my handsome grandsons, Darby Marshall and Devin Doyle, and to the man who encouraged me to write one more book, my faithful friend of forty five years, Joe Hollis McDaniel. He and his sweet wife, Ann, have welcomed us into their Alabama farm home time and time again and refreshed our spirits and encouraged our hearts.

And with special thanks to the Pleasant View Church families from 1953 to today who have supported and encouraged me with their love, their prayers, their patience and their resources, especially the Beesleys, the Wilds, the Dixons, the Robbins, the Tempests, the Moncriefs, and the Jones. And to Bill and Patty Robertson whose help I could not have done without, also Terry Wick Machowski, who presented me the picture of the Sentinel, the cover photo, and to Daniel, my son, who patiently did those little computer chores I find so difficult. And lastly, to Joe Chambers, who added to my information on the Willard Reynolds family.

GENERATION CHART FOR WILBUR REYNOLDS

Siblings**
Charles 1910*
Harry 1912*   Elvia Muster Hastings*   Will F Randall+

Siblings+
Waldo 1902+
Ralph 1904+
Earnest 1915#+
Elizabeth 916#+

(second wife)   (second husband)

Mary 1913*
Virgie 1915*
Tressie 1917*

Stella 1918#+

Robert 1921*   Wm Edwin Reynolds
                  August 1878-1930
                  m. Nov 28, 1901#
                  m. April 13, 1910*

Louvina Ziegler#
Jan 21, 1882-1976

                          Wilbur Reynolds#
                          B: Dec 17, 1902
                          m. Feb 24, 1947
                          D: Feb 19, 1968
                          (wife)Nora Detamore

Merritt Reynolds
Sept 1856-1938
m. Feb 1877

Charles Ziegler
June 1854-1915
m. Apr 1881

                  Mary Ellen Renn   Sarah C. Arney
                  Nov 1854-1919   Apr 10, 1859-1937

Joseph Reynolds   Enoch Renn   Isaac Arney   Isaac Ziegler
Feb 1835-1920   Feb 1832-1901   Oct 1815-1888   Jan 1821-1901
m. Aug 18, 1855   m. Jan 1, 1854   m. Aug 1857   m. 1840s

Almira Cheever   Rebecca Thurston   Diantha Davis   Sarah Schneider
June 1835-1903   Feb 1839-1924   Feb 1832-1905   Oct 1821-1907

David Reynolds   Henry Renn   Daniel Ziegler
1791-1874   1802-1887
m. March 1819   m.   m.
Sarah Penwell   Rachel Campbell   Catherine ?
1798-1861   1802-1880
W. F. Cheever   Sylvanus Thurston   Charles Davis   Samuel Schneider
1814-1874   1806-1852   1795-1871
m. June 1834   m.   m. Dec. 1822   m.
Amelia Jones   Lucinda Beers   Sarah Davis   Sarah Binder

Wilbur's great-great-great grandparents that we know of include Abner Cheever (Vermont), George and Prudance Jones (VA), Robert and Elizabeth Campbell (PA), Moses Thurston and Catherine Bottenhomer, and Eli and Susan Beers (PA) and Nathaniel Davis and Margaret Murley (VA/ KY). We think David Reynolds' father was Joseph. The Reynolds family came from New York, the Renns and Thurstons, Ziegler/Schneider family and Arneys from Pennsylvania, the Jones and Davis families from Virginia.

Contents

Psalms 16

The land You have given me
Is a pleasant land
What a wonderful inheritance!

I will bless the Lord who guides me:
Even at night my heart instructs me.

I know the Lord is always with me
I will not be shaken
For He is right beside me.

You will show me the way of life,
Granting me the joy of your presence
And the pleasure of living with you
Forever.

Introduction

A woman screamed! That, of course, was not unusual in the labor delivery area of the small country hospital at Seymour, Indiana in the year 1947, but this did not sound like a scream of pain, but of fear. Then the screamer cried out, "My baby, my baby," and the two nurses on duty fell over each other getting to the young woman, hoping that what they were thinking had not occurred. They were short handed because of the stormy day, a day of slashing rain, lighting, and rumbling thunder, thunderstorm after thunderstorm rolling through the southeastern Indiana countryside. Because of the staff shortage, the nurses had taken the young woman, who had checked in not twenty minutes ago, to the toilet and left her for a few minutes to check on other patients. Now they hurried to discover their worse fears confirmed. Yet they were professionals, and they quickly did what needed to be done. Throwing towels on the floor, they lowered the young woman to the floor, and while one nurse gave her attention to the woman and the cord, the other snatched the baby girl from the toilet and with great relief, after clearing her passages, listened to her cry. It was 6:26 P.M., April 20, 1947.

A few minutes later, both the father and the old country doctor, D. W. Matthews, arrived on the floor, both too late to be of any help. The doctor had actually been parking his car because he had insisted on driving the couple to the hospital, thinking their old car would not make it in the storm. And since he had not delivered a baby that day, the doctor refused to present a bill for delivery. He did accept payment seventeen months later, a payment of thirty-five dollars in dimes, for the delivery of their second child, born at Aunt Pete's in Lovett Township, because that young woman refused to trust another hospital with one of her babies.

Thus begins the saga that will include eight generations, five before the birth of these two children and two afterwards that were part of the unfolding drama of the lives of ordinary people who left New York and Pennsylvania and Virginia and ventured westward in the early 1800s to make their homes along the streams of Jennings County, Indiana. The twisted roots of their lives come together in the lives of Loralyn and

Danny Reynolds, who grew up on the banks of the Wyaloosing in the 1950's and 60's, a short few miles from where their g g g grandfather, Henry Renn settled on the Wyaloosing in 1853, and across the creek from where Loralyn and Danny played, their great, great, great uncle, Eli Thurston, had raised his family in the 1870' and 80's on a small farm he bought when he returned from the Civil War. Within a few square miles, there can be found in five small country cemeteries, the stones that acknowledge direct ancestors. Within these same square miles are the farms once owned by Renn, Thurston, Campbell, Reynolds, Cheever, and Jones ancestors. The streams they settled on, besides the Wyaloosing, include Sand Creek and Fish Creek. The creeks of Wimple, Rattail, and Bear Creek also bear some mention. And farther south, and east you will find the Muscatatuck River and Pleasant Run and Brush Creek where the Davis brothers settled and Crooked Creek and Goose Creek that ran through the Ziegler and Arney farms. In that section of the county, it is common to find ancestors at cemeteries at Brush Creek and Butlerville, but most of the southern ancestors are buried at the larger cemetery at Vernon. You will also find members of this family at the cemetery at North Vernon.

Even though these stories are written for my family, especially my grandsons, it is my hope that I will have written clearly enough that family researchers (in other words, distant, distant cousins) can be helped by this information.

Even though I will document as accurately as possible, much of my research was based on interviews and letters, which may or may not be historically accurate. But the fun is in the journey, and however wrong or right I may be in interpreting my family, they are real to me, and I have to believe, overall, they were very much like me, men and women who valued family, faith, work and the land.

I hope you enjoy, at least parts of "The Banks of the Wyaloosing". It is definitely more than a history of a family, but a work of becoming and overcoming, of lessons learned, of growth achieved.

Please understand, this is a collage of stories and written sketches. There is no set pattern, and it is deliberately so. It fits the personality of the author.

It is not a book to be read from page one to ending but to pick and choose as interest dictates. Scan the entries and taste and enjoy or lay aside and bemoan the fact that you bought it.

Loralyn Reynolds April of 2014

Acknowledgement

Credit for the maps used goes to actual surveys by J. M. Lathrop and J.H. Summers, and published by D.J. Lake, <u>The 1884 Atlas of Jennings County</u>, Indiana and reproduced by the Our Heritage whose representative gladly gave permission for their use. Thank you.

Instructions

To use this book for research, please note that the HN: stands for historical notes. This is information that can be confirmed from census records, recorded obituaries, other documents and at times reliable family letters. The genealogical charts are all based on documentation, census records, marriage and death records, newspaper clippings, family letters.

The Sentinel

Branches are missing.
Buffeted by wind and rain.
The Sycamore still stands,
Sentinel above the meandering creek.

It was there
When I was a girl.
It is the only tree
I remember so clearly
In that wooded playground
Of my childhood.

Those woods a perfect place
To play Robin Hood
And picnic on a flat rock.

We did not fear the snakes
Nor were careful enough
But once in awhile
One would surprise us,
Usually lying on the old gravel road.
And in the play of shadow and sunlight
Of the overhanging trees
One often thought a snake a stick
Or a stick a snake.

What we did fear
Happened anyway!
We grew up
And went away.

On
the
Banks
of
the
Wyaloosing

A Legacy of LOVE and FAITH,
a Whisper of HOPE

In an Italian ristorante, high on a cliff, overlooking the Bay of Naples, I have sat, laughing with friends, enjoying a bowl of carbonara topped with pancetta and onion. I have climbed the leaning tower of Pisa and have listened to a gondolier raise his voice in song in Venice, and in Florence I gazed upon the magnificent sculpture, Michelangelo's "David". I have enjoyed the quiet serenity of Assisi and the clamoring noises of the open market in Naples and Pintemare, and I have stood in awe in the Sistene Chapel. I have known breathtaking moments as I first caught a glimpse of the majestic snow-covered Alps and felt the pervading sadness when we visited Dachau. In the lovely little German town of Berchtesgaden, I felt so at home in our favorite restaurant there, "The Bear" where we enjoyed schnitzel and strudel; and even more at home in the village of Herrenberg, where our friends, Helmut and Beatte lived with their two pretty little girls. I would stroll down the narrow streets, and, oh, I can still remember the fragrance of freshly baked breads from the local bakery, wonderful loaves of both dark and light; my favorite, a dark bread filled with sunflower seeds. And in an old stone church, we worshiped with them, and although we did not understand the language, the hymns we recognized.

Oh, we saw Munich and Paris and Augsburg and as much of Rome as we could devour; we traveled in the Netherlands and Belgian and in one of those places, our host insisted on fixing us a Dutch pancake, baked in the oven. We took a whirlwind tour of London, after a troop plane carried us over the English Channel from our home base in Naples. Our English Bread and Breakfast hosts loved having a baby in the house. In Scotland, we barely missed the Queen Mother, who happened to take Tea at the same place we had ventured to for the same reason. And in Scotland, a local lady insisted on talking to me at the train station, while I nursed my baby, and even though I was sure she was speaking English and I was as polite as I could be, I had no idea of any word she spoke. She was delightful, just dialectical. And in my mind's eye, I can still picture the pastoral scenes of Scotland, sheep dotting green hills and the wash hanging in the kitchen of the friends with whom we stayed. They had lost a son and were still grieving. Now I understand.

But if our three years in Europe had given us no time to travel, we would have still been enriched by the friendships of those Italian people who shared their homes and lives with us. I never dreamed I would travel like I have done. It was interesting and I am glad for those experiences, and the credit for the travel goes to Charles, the man who made life interesting, who loved to travel, who liked to meet people, who thrived on new experiences, the man I was married to for twenty years, the father of my children, the man I once loved, and sometimes hated, the man who I will never fully understand, but can still appreciate for many things he did give to me. I loved him for his commitment to God and his family, but I hated the moody spells, the times he wouldn't talk to us, for the times in those twenty years that he tried to send us 'home', just wanted to get us out of his hair. He was still willing to support us, and remain in name a married man. He loved us, but in his own words, he was not a very loving man nor responsive to the touchy, feely woman he chose to marry. As a father, he was sometimes wonderful and sometimes emotionally withdrawn. Being respected was more important to Charles than being loved, which is one reason he became more and more a workaholic. As the saying goes, 'He had his work; I had my babies'. I did and do respect him for his work ethic, but I so needed a little bit of him and now I understand he couldn't give it, at least not to me. Most of my life, I have brought out the best in the people around me, but once in awhile, there is someone whom I seem to trigger the worse in. Sadly, one of those people was Charles. In a sad cycle of rejections, we pulled away from each other, even though there were still good things about our marriage. Ultimately, the good times would get shorter and the bad times longer.

You must understand that we were both Christian believers and had prayed about our relationship. Obviously, we failed to hear God say, "Wait, it won't work"!

It was my childhood legacy growing up on the Wyaloosing that helped me survive the marriage and painstakingly rebuild my shattered life, and recapture, at least, some of my broken dreams. It was a legacy of faith and love and hope. And I'm going to tell you about it. Whether you listen or read is up to you.

Our (my brother, Danny and myself) legacy is intertwined with warm summer days of hay drying in the field, green corn fields and bushy soybeans, chasing fireflies, the laughter of children swimming in the Wyloosing, and skating on her ice in the winter, a legacy that includes snow in winter, inches of it; redbud and dogwood blooming in the spring, and a myriad of wildflowers along the creeks and roadsides and that delicious delicacy of the shaded woods, the morel mushroom. The fall of the year found the southern Indiana hills covered with riotous colors of reds and gold and yellow, oranges and rust, and splotches of burgundy.

Our legacy was laced with poverty and pride, love and commitment to family, helping your neighbor, respecting the land, serious work ethics, and acceptance of life as it came to you. Make the best of what you are given. Have dreams, but maturity is reached when you realize that all dreams do not come true, and there is no perfect place and no perfect person and no perfect job. It is maturity when we learn to live day by day, making the most of the gifts we have been given, and the day is ours. It is maturity when we realize we are not the center of the world and we must consider the needs of others. It is maturity when we realize we have a choice to sink in despair or be an over comer when hard things come into our lives. It is maturity when one realizes that everyone has their share of heartaches and griefs and broken dreams. It is maturity when one realizes there is no right way to do the wrong thing, but God is a God of grace and mercy and he does forgive when we botch up our lives and go and ask Him to take the tangled threads and make something beautiful out of our lives. It is maturity when you learn to praise God in all things.

It is maturity when you don't walk off the stage before the song is finished.

Oh, but there are times I wanted to! Depression has danced its way in and out of my life-my fault. It happens when I forget all the above things, when I want more than I have, when I forget that peace is mine when I can thank God for all He has given and for all He has taken away. There are periods in my life that I have had that peace, and periods when I blew it. Now I am struggling to achieve that peace stage while I deal with Parkinson Disease and disability and retirement, an empty nest and the lost of friends and family. And during this time, if I am not careful, I let the sad times of the past and the mistakes I've made creep in and make me forget what I have had and what I still have.

I must accept that I am who I am, that I am where I am, and that God is not finished with my life. I cannot go back and marry another man, create another life, make another series of mistakes, and grasp a few achievements. I have been greatly loved, by family, by friends. Most of all, I have experienced God's love, and I like Him close. I hope to feel His love always.

I have always been very serious about my faith in God, and equated morality with my faith. Now, I am not so sure. Yes, God is a God of righteousness. Don't get me wrong, I believe that. But moreover, I believe He is a God of love and mercy, and when our hearts are committed to Him, He is with us when we fail. He understands when we tried so hard not to fail, but did anyway, and then he picks us up and sets us back on the path we are suppose to be on. Oh, but I so wanted to be good all the time, and do something really great for God and people. Yet I have only managed to be good some of the time, only loving some of the time, only patient some of the time. I raised three wonderful kids, wonderful, partly because of me, and partly despite me. The greatest loss of my life is to have one of them snatched away from me at twenty-two. There will always be missing him, wishing he'd call on the phone, wishing I could hold him again, scratch his back, cook his favorite meal, just be with him.

Yet, that loss I can live with. I know I will go home to him someday instead of him coming home as I expected in 1996 ("November," he said. He said, "I'll be home in November, you can count on me. I'll be home in November. You know I know the way." Yes, he knew the way, where love and family waited.) Yes, the boy I had endured five major surgeries with, watched grow to proud manhood, beloved and loving.

Oh, God, it isn't fair! But I know I am not the first mother to lose a son, and sadly, I will not be the last.

Yes, my life's greatest loss was my son, but the hurt and grief of not being loved and cherished in my marriage sometimes still troubles at me, and I suppose if I had remarried and finally had all I had missed, I would be able to let it go. I had hoped to find someone to love me and remarry. It didn't happen, and now my health is in the way. I spent too many years blaming Charles for our poor marriage. (That only kept me from moving forward). That does not mean I do not hold him responsible. There is a fine line there, but holding someone responsible is not the same as blame. But as has been stated by those wiser than I, who can understand the complexities of the inner workings of any person? Yet whether it was my fault, his fault, or no body's fault, it never became a true marriage of oneness. The good times got shorter and the bad times got longer. But I stayed, and stayed too long, just trying to make it work. Sometimes I stayed for the right reasons and sometimes for the wrong reasons. When one makes a mistake as serious as marrying the wrong man, and then compounding it with children, when does one leave? I finally knew it was over when I stood at the edge of the darkness, and knew I could not keep trying, that if we stayed together, I would leave the way I feared the most, consumed by the darkness of a nervous or emotional breakdown. To climb out of the depression and find myself again, and work through my issues, and keep a presence of some sense about me so I would not be a total loss to my children: that was my goal. With the best of intentions to live a good and holy life, I had now a life tangled and twisted, and I struggled with despair. But God spoke to my heart, and He speaks again and again. He told me He was with me, and together we would find our way through the tangles until my life made some sense again. He has not left me, and He is the God that is healing me. My heart is so grateful for His faithfulness. I just wanted to be so much more!

SO here are more glimpses into our childhood that God used to give me a foundation for building and rebuilding a life.

I grew to womanhood along the banks of the Wyaloosing, a winding creek that begins in Decatur County and winds its way down to Jennings and then empties into Sand Creek at Scipio. Two smaller creeks empty into the Wyloosing in Jennings. They are Bear Creek and Rattail. In the 1870s after he came back from the Civil War, my great-great-great Uncle, Eli Thurston, bought a farm that lay between the Rattail and the Wyaloosing, across the creek from land my dad bought in the 1950s. Everywhere I go, within five miles from where I grew up, are farms that my ancestors bought back in the 1800s, farms on the Wyloosing and on Sandcreek and on Fish Creek, and yes, on Wimple. Now those farms are owned by someone else, but I am here because long ago those pioneer men and women with the names of Thurston and Renn and Cheever and Jones and Campbell and of course, Reynolds, left Pennsylvania and New York and Vermont and Virginia and they came to Indiana. Some of their children stayed and some of their grandchildren and now I can count seven and eight generations of my father's people that have lived here. But moreover, I am here because I chose to come back as my father chose to stay. Our roots are here and we are a rooted type of people. The country cemeteries as well as the cemeteries at Vernon and North Vernon abound with family, dating back almost two hundred years. Overall, they were families that stayed together, worked together, prayed together. They loved the land and clung tenaciously to it. They wanted better for their children, more land, a better education, church in the community, and still a faith to live by and a hope to die by.

It was with that ethic that I was raised, but our lives are shaped by many things, yes, including our families and our environment, and also including the geographical aspect. Other shaping factors include the political and national trends and events, the justices and injustices of each generation. It has seemed important to me at this point in my life to look at all this and pass down these stories to my grandchildren. They may or may not appreciate them. However, it is my hope that in reading they will be more at peace with not who they could have been, but simply who they are. I think that in time, we all must reach that place.

On the Banks of the Wyaloosing 1947-2014

Memoirs of Danny and Loralyn Reynolds

(1968)

He was dying. She wanted to deny it but death would come anyway. For days she did not cry. Then two days after his funeral, she took out his clothes to sort. She was alone in the house he had built in the fifties here on the Wyaloosing, here where she had grown up with the wild flowers and the woods he so loved.

Most of his clothes were worn overalls and flannel shirts, few pieces worth giving away. Then she pressed the flannel to her cheeks and began to cry. Unabashedly, the tears came, with loud broken sobs. She soaked the shirt she held, and even though the shirt was clean, she could smell again the smell of him, the mixture of sweat and tobacco after a ten hour day in the mill and a cow milked.

She had been the apple of his eye, her daddy's little girl. He had nearly worshiped his children. Losing him at twenty and nineteen (her brother, Danny's age at the time) was hard but they would always carry the special feeling of being loved and cherished and they could always look in the mirror and see his face.

In her mind's eye, she could still see him, and through the years would pull him back to remember. There was usually a stubble on his face. He tended to shave only on Saturdays and for funerals. He took a bath in the creek once or twice a year whether he needed it or not. His hair was already white when his children were born and they never remember him having teeth. He liked his coffee three times a day and no snacks, ate eggs every morning except Sunday. His skin was tough and leathery from years of working outside, and his eyes were a shade of blue, turning gray blue when angry. He could look daggers at a person and convey displeasure with someone without a word. He was firm with his children but fair as his grandparents had been with him. He sucked a pipe as much as he smoked one. He could be outgoing and engaging but liked his times of solitude, rose early each morning to have time to himself before the day began, liked long walks in the woods and along the creek. It was not unusual to find him talking to himself or maybe he was praying, even though he never bore evidence of a churchman, went only when cajoled by his children. He was most definitely committed to caring for his family and was a good neighbor. Bib overalls were his choice of dress. There was always long underwear in winter, and winter meant a small bottle of whiskey secured in the upper cabinet, to be used only in case of a severe cold or attack of influenza. He rarely missed a day of work for any reason. Even when flooding across the road prevented him from driving to work, he would walk through the woods.

As to other likes, he loved country music, square dancing, the Friday night fights (I went to sleep many a night with the sound of the Friday night fights as my lullaby, knowing my dad was hunched over the old radio). He didn't seem to be very fond of hugs. You had to hug him quick before he complained. He was a meat and potatoes man, liked a good pie. He cussed with every other word and smoked even on his death bed. As a young man, he had attended church and given his heart to God, but as an adult attended church sparingly and took some of his heart back. Shortly before his death, he gave back to God his wasted body and saddened soul. The Lord and the devil may have had an argument over his soul, but I believe he waits for us in a better place.

(From Loralyn's pen—January of 2014)

It was in the early 1950's "that our folks bought this small tract of land along the Wyaloosing. Here they built a house, raised chickens, had a cow, and raised two kids grown to adulthood. They were, by anyone's standards, a poorly matched couple, but somehow, they combined their individual strengths and gave my brother and I a fairly good foundation—one with a strong work ethic and a strong sense of family. As a family we had our share of dysfunctionality but even though our family life could have been better, it could have been very, very much worse. We are both grateful for what we were given and I have come to believe that the same family that shares its weaknesses with us is the same family that shares its strengths and we can choose to overcome or be overcome. We have chosen to be over comers, like our parents before us and many of those who went before them.

You must know, to understand this story that Wilbur Reynolds, our father, was born with a crippled left hand and a partial left lung. Throughout his life, there were many who had known him for years and did not know of his hand. That was because he worked like a man with two good hands. He had been raised chiefly by his grandparents and Charles and Sarah Arney Ziegler did not allow him to feel sorry for himself, and he was expected to do the chores other boys did and play the games they played. A story oft told had to do with 'The Bully'. Our dad was perhaps seven or eight years old at the time, and the school year started with this kid picking on Dad. It got worse as Dad tried to avoid the kid, and the kid began to get rougher as bullies will do. When his grandfather realized what was happening, he sat my father down, and gave him the talk of his life. He told him this situation was not going to continue, that my father was to fight back, and with the way he had been taught to work and to play, as with two good hands. As an added incentive, my great grandfather promised my father a spanking if he came home again in a beaten up state. The next day as my father walked home with his friends, the bully came running along and gave my dad a shove. Before anyone took another step, my father threw down his book bag, turned on the bully with a vengeance, had him on the ground in seconds and sitting on him, beat him with both hands. My dad's friends pulled him off, afraid now for the other kid. My dad spat out, as he rounded on the boy whose nose was bleeding and his eye beginning to bruise, "Never, never, never again!" The shocked kid shook his dazed head in agreement, and that was the end of that story.

Other stories that I will be sharing will show you my father's overcoming spirit. His motto was "If there is a will, there is a way".

He was also a teacher, not a teacher with a degree, but a man who liked to have his children with him, teaching them the things he knew. I can still hear the laughter, as in my mind's eye, I see two barefooted children running over sun warmed, freshly turned earth, stopping now and then to pick up a fishing worm. Sometimes I can still experience the feelings of bare toes in that soft, crumbly earth, and remember the sun warm on my head, the sights and sounds of early summer, the exhalation of being a happy child on a perfect garden 'putting in' day. Planting the garden was always an exciting time, a family together time, a time that built pleasant memories for children who still indulge the child within them and who still love to grow things like their daddy did.

He taught us how to fish, how to use a gun and to hunt, but moreover, he taught us a love of the woods and the incredible silence that comes just before dawn, just before the birds begin to sing. It is still my favorite time of day. He also showed us the marvel of the tasty morel and named the many trees. There were walnut, beech, oak, maple, poplar and buckeye trees in our woods, as well as the flowering redbud and the dogwood and paw paws, also a hazelnut tree and some cedar. Usually there was a cedar right for Christmas, but one year there wasn't, so Dad asked our neighbor, Jim Wilds if we could hunt one on his land. Jim agreed. We were older by then, in our early teens, and Dad sent us for the tree, whereas it had usually been a threesome activity.

The day we went, snow was on the ground, and it began snowing after we left the house, a soft, slow coming down kind of snow. After looking on our side of the creek, we decided to cross the creek and look on the other side. I assume the creek was frozen over. I don't remember, but it must have been. So we crossed the creek and kept looking, not finding what we wanted. We were getting tired and frustrated. Then all of a sudden, we came upon a lovely group of fir trees. We chose one, cut it down and began the trek home dragging our tree. About a third of the way home, as we pulled our tree over a fence, did I began to doubt that we had found the tree on Jim's land. Danny was disgusted with me. He was cold and just wanted to get home. He certainly was not going to go back and double check the area we had found the tree in. Hadn't we played in these woods for years? Didn't we know where Jim's woods ended? Apparently not, but it would be years before I knew the truth. We drug our tree home leaving a trail a blind man could follow and Mr. Scroggins was not blind. The owner of the trees discovered the lost of his tree the same day and followed the trail to where it ended at our house. He then turned around and went back home, only sharing the story with our mutual friend, Jim Wilds, who got a chuckle out of it.

You see, in a small community like ours, everyone knew everyone, and Mr. Scroggins knew we weren't bad kids, and that in all probability, we had not stolen a Christmas tree even though technically we did. It was years later after Mr. Scroggins' death that Jim shared the side of the story he knew. And all through those years, Mr. Scroggins greeted me warmly at church as if I were one of his favorite people, not the little thief he knew me to be. I thank God again and again for the joy of growing up in a community where people cared about people.

I guess, by now, you have figured out that Jim Wilds was one of those caring people. Jim cared deeply about his neighbors and his church. He was a man who would never have taught a Sunday School class, but lived his faith by his actions. He and my dad were friends. He was one of the men I called the night my daddy died and he came without hesitation. He was also a pallbearer for Daddy, and I still remember his walking down the aisle of the church toward the casket, and the tears rolling down his ruggedly handsome face. Yes, he loved my dad, as much as the feisty little redhead he married loved me. She was the one who urged my dad to bring his family to church. He had been stopping at their farm for eggs because there was a sign out and our hens had gone on strike. She was a new Christian at the time, and had begun to substitute teach the children's class. Finally Dad did take us to church, and soon Betty was teaching the children's class fulltime. She learned to love teaching so much that she kept graduating with her class, and it was she who walked with me down that aisle of our little country church four years later when I gave my heart to Christ. Our friendship was nearly the journey of a lifetime. I was six when it began. It went on for nearly sixty years.

It was Jim and Betty Wilds who sold Dad and Mom the ten acres on the Wyaloosing in the 1950's when they found out Dad wanted to move back to the creek. We had lived on the creek from the time I was six months old to when I was five, then had moved a few miles away on Bear Creek where we rented an old federally style farm house with a big barn and double corncrib. It was fun there with a barn full of hay to play in and blackberry patches galore in the pasture. We always got more chiggers than berries, but we'd do it again the next year. Our grandmother with her ruffled sun bonnet would come out from her place at Vernon and usher us out to help pick. She helped my mother can the berries. She also would make a big pot of blackberry dumplings. Um, Um, good! There we had an orchard and chickens as well as our milk cows, a Jersey named Bell and a Guernsey named June. Dad milked, sometimes selling the milk and sometimes separating the milk and the cream and selling just the cream. If a family gathering was to be held, like it was once or twice a year at our house, Dad would save the cream for the homemade ice cream. Great uncles and aunts would busy themselves with the ice cream making, women making up the mixture and the men cranking away, jawing as they did. After a good deal of cranking and story telling and local politics, the ice cream would be left to set up while the spread was devoured. Everyone brought something and there was always plenty to eat. Usually these gatherings included Aunt Dona and Aunt Ivan and Aunt Pete and their families. I call them the Jennings County aunts. Sometimes Aunt Mary and some of her family would come down from Marion. These were my mother's people, the Detamores. Grandpa Detamore was usually there, too but he was also often at our house for Sunday dinner, and when we were little, he wrestled with us and played with us by the hour. He was a good grandfather, at least to Danny and me. We shared a special closeness until the day he died and maybe we still do. One of my favorite memories is standing on his feet and looking through the fence rails at the county fair to watch the horse races. Watching the harness races with Grandpa at the fair was a yearly event.

Back of the house was a cistern of which we were very respectful. There was also an orchard with several varieties of apples, and chicken houses. There is no greater joy in the spring than to watch an old biddy with several fluffy yellow chicks following her. But one stormy morning, a tornado came through and blew down one chicken house and took part of our roof. Mom was scared to death and Dad was at the sawmill when it hit. She contained her fears and appearing calm, took us to the bedroom where there was only one window. We all lay across the bed and colored. Danny and I were unaware we were in any danger until Dad pounded on the door. He was obviously one relieved man to find us safe. He took us to the living room window that looked out on the orchard and chicken houses. We saw that it had flattened our chicken house and our poor chickens. Our favorite apple trees were mangled.

In the house there, Mom still cooked on a wood range. We all slept in the same large bedroom because the two upstairs rooms were too cold in winter and too hot in summer. They made good playrooms and Dad stored his sugar cured ham there.

Other special memories of the years on Bear Creek include getting off the school bus on a fine spring day and walking the quarter mile lane to the house and singing at the top of our lungs, 'Swing Low, Sweet Chariot'. Yes, Danny, too. Winter snow days found us enjoying the hills with the sled that had actually been our father's as a boy. He had given it to his nephew Bill, and Bill returned it when we were old enough to enjoy it. When he came, Grandpa would take walks with us and shared some chores. Once we were filling up the water bucket at the pump, and I got too close to the handle and got a bump on my head. My grandfather was stricken, but we both survived.

My dad and grandfather got along fine as long as they didn't live together. When I was born, my dad and mom had been living with him on his farm near Lovett. We stayed another six months after my birth, but it was a far piece from there to the sawmill on Wimple Creek where dad worked for his brother-in-law, Archie Robbins. SO when Osa Wilds, offered Dad a rent free house near the mill, he snapped up the offer, especially since he and Grandpa were not getting along so well. Grandpa wept when we left. He had been used to coming in each afternoon and giving me my sugar bottle. He loved holding me at that stage, whereas Dad was scared to hold me until I was older.

When we moved into the cabin on the Wyaloosing, it was October and the Indiana hills were afame with color. My mother stated that one could have thrown a cat through the cracks of the old log cabin. The rent free stipulation hinged on Dad fixing up the place, and he had to get to work fast. The old cabin had housed many families, and several Wilds' babies had been born there. Through the years, after we left it, it housed several other families before it gave up. It was there I learned to crawl, to walk and there at eighteen months, I scared my dad badly when I fell into his saw. He thought he had cut my fingers off. There was so much blood! But it was really only the tip of one finger. Uncle Archie and Dad took me in to Dr. Matthews (the doctor who didn't deliver me) who calmed my father and stitched up my finger. Through the years, many children have asked me about my funny finger, "What happen to your finger?' For some reason with great glee, I answer solemnly, "My father cut it off." They always gasp and get really big eyed. Then I grin and explain what really happen.

It was soon after this that I decided to run away. I got as far as the swinging bridge, and when my dad caught up with me, he switched my little backside all the way back to the cabin. Living on the creek was a wonderful experience, but the creek could be dangerous and it had to be respected. One time Dad sat up all night watching the flood waters come up as far as the porch. If it had come farther, he would have taken his little family up over the hill to neighbors, but it was a far piece. The Wyaloosing was usually a pretty stream, and behaved herself and stayed in her banks and gurgled over the rocks in the ford. At that stage, the sound was musically. It was a joy to drift off to sleep on a summer night listening to the song of the creek. Besides the gift of song, the creek offered up good fishing and one year provided for our Christmas. Our dad trapped fur bearing animals, checking the trap lines sometimes in the dark with a lantern, after a long day in the mill. He sold the furs to Couchman. In the fifties Couchman was the name in North Vernon that went with furs. I never met the man, but I will always remember his name,

The creek ran between the road and the cabin. I was at least two when this next incident happened.

It was a lovely summer day and my young mother finished up her chores and set out to visit the neighbors. The only way to cross was to ford the creek or cross on the swinging bridge. Sun sparkled on the water rippling over the rocks in the ford. Mom didn't swim and she was afraid of the ford, even on such a pretty day. She had crossed the bridge many times just the way she planned to do it this day. She put a diaper in her dress, picked up the baby and took me by the hand. We walked across the yard and begin to cross the bridge. Half way across, a slat broke and my mother's foot went through. She could not dislodge it. She could not put down the baby and she couldn't let go of my hand. At first she felt panicky, but no, that would not do. Finally she had me hold onto her dress while she again tried to get her foot out. There was no need to waste her breath in yelling because the neighbors lived up a long lane and would not hear her. She could not wait for a car to come along. Sometimes a car didn't come by for hours at a time. And it would be hours before my father came home from work.

The baby was getting restless and her leg was growing numb. Finally, with her heart in her throat, she said to me. "Listen." You must let go of my hand and you must walk very slowly down the middle of the bridge and climb the hill and cross the road and go up the lane and get Johnny and bring him back to help me." And that, according to my mother, is what I did. I crossed the bridge, climbed the hill, went across the old gravel road, and up the lane, and brought back a blind man to help my mother.

What do you think??? Did I have help that day? Did an angel walk with me?

Each of our lives is a story and our story is made up of many stories. Those stories reveal our God at work in our lives. Sometimes we recognize Him and give him thanks and sometimes we fail to see his hand, especially when it is a hard time, or a time of darkness.

I love the 139 Psalm. I believe that this affirms that God knows us before we are born and He is already at work arranging and rearranging our lives in order to bring us where He wants us to be. That does not throw out free will. We still have the freedom to make wrong choices and we do. At least most of us do. It only indicates that God is an all knowing GOD. He knows the choices we will make and He knows when He has to come and pull us back to Himself and get us back on the right path.

It is not unusual for God to provide not only people and angels in our lives to help and protect us but animals as well. There is a favorite picture of me sitting on a blanket with Mutt behind me. Mutt belonged to the neighbors, but was more oft at our house. He was always very protective of me. Yet the funniest Mutt story doesn't involve me. It goes this way. Mom had baked two cherry pies and set them outside to cool on the window ledge. They both disappeared. The metal pans were found in the nearby cornfield. The dog was discovered with sticky fur.

Now I am not going to share every single story that tells me God is always at work in my life. They are way too many, but I will share a few and I hope it will help you see that He has been at work in your own life. Now as a child, although I loved my parents and appreciated them, I really thought God could have done a better job in the set of parents He gave me. Now I know they were the parents I was suppose to have and I'm ever so grateful for their influence on my life and the support they always offered.

By the time I was twelve I was talking about college. I didn't realize we were too poor for me to go. I just thought that was what God wanted me to do. Another lady in the church, Ann Dixon, took me to visit her college and when I did, I knew I had to go to Asbury. From a practical standpoint, it was not a good decision. It would have been cheaper to have attended an Indiana college. But God provided, even in the face of my dad's advancing cancer. He was in the hospital when I graduated from high school. When he came home, we talked about college and he told me to go find a summer job. I found two, and he took me to both jobs and came and picked me up. So off to college I went that fall, with my earnings from two jobs, two small scholarships, and a few twenties from friends at church. I managed to graduate in the usual four years with only one loan my senior year. (Uncle Archie went with me to procure and co-signed) My dad had died my junior year, but he knew our dream was in sight, and he had finally given in, as he put it, shortly before his death, and gave what was left of himself to God.

We grew up poor, but we also recognized that there were other families with less. Our parents were poorly educated, but both hard workers. They taught us a serious work ethic, that family is important and you take care of your own, and that you sacrifice your own happiness for your children, and if your marriage is not good, you endure it. You accept life as it comes to you and you make the best of what you have been given. Also, you help your neighbor whether you like him or not. And my dad was adamant that we finish high school and he didn't like my boyfriend. Eventually I broke up with the boyfriend because we had an argument about college, but he never left my heart. We were too young, and too self willed to compromise. I did stay close to his family who had encouraged me in my faith.

Now I am getting off the subject. Back to business. At Asbury, I continued to be a serious student and got involved with service projects. I made friendships that have lasted to this day. My senior year, I was accepted by the Methodist Board of Missions to serve in the Kentucky mountains. When I decided to get married, they didn't want me. I still have a pull to the mountain areas of Kentucky. I had thought about finding a summer project there after I retired, but I am not sure now whether my health will allow it.

Now as a young Christian, I had grown rapidly and then at marriage, first job and first baby, I seemed to stop growing. I realize on looking back that it was those cares of the world that Jesus talks about in the parable of the soils. I was letting day to day life choke out my relationship with Christ. So for the next few years, I saw little growth in my life, and I felt like I was acting a part when it came to my Christian life and I didn't like it. During that time, my second child was born, and with a birth defect that meant surgery after surgery. I worried. I was depressed. Then when I thought things were at their lowest ebb, I got busy and things changed. I went back to morning devotions. I held a Bible study in my home. I took lots of Vitamin B and went on a diet. And God pulled me through that time and helped me grow and other people were helped too. We'd been talking about separating, but instead our marriage flourished, and we had the best two years of our marriage and family life. I foolishly thought then that God had us on course and the marriage would continue to improve and my spiritual life would be advancing. Wrong!!

After our transfer to Italy, Charles became career oriented again, and his moody spells became longer. I struggled with depression over his behavior, and we began to discuss separation again. Then Daniel came and things were better for a short time. But the marriage was failing

21

and counseling could not work when only one person tried. I had been taught you stay no matter what but I finally realized I would end up like my grandmother who suffered from manic depressive symptoms. I had to get out. My dream of a happy and loving marriage was shattered. It felt at that time that all hell was unleashed to destroy me, but God sent some very special people to help me through that time of severe depression and yes, oppression, and He helped me rebuild my life.

Just as I felt like I was experiencing some real healing and a bit of happiness, my middle child was killed in an accident. He was serving in the United States Air Force in Japan. I felt like I had just regained some of my balance after being dashed by a wave, and now an even greater wave was washing over me. Nothing is harder than losing a child. But again, God surrounded me with His presence, gave me friends and family to help me through this. There are too many to mention by name but one must be mentioned. That is my friend, Katrina Roberts Miller, friends since high school and the one to insist I persist in obtaining a social work job at The Muscatatuck State Developmental Center for adults with disabilities. It was the most rewarding work experience of my life. The entire week, from the time we heard of Clay's death, to the time I left for his funeral, Katrina left work and came and sat on the front porch swing with me. We just sat. She gave me the gift of silence and sat there and shared my pain. My Clay and her Ryan were the same age and had enjoyed the times they were together.

One friend who helped I had never met. I just call her 'she'. Because the little piece of the land on the Wyaloosing is a place I feel close to God, I went there often after Clay's death. For months, I either felt numb or had bouts of agonizing grief. I would go out to the land and follow the deer trail down to the water. I never saw the deer, but it was as if an affinity developed. On an unusually lovely day in spring, almost ten months after Clay's death, when the wildflowers were blooming and the redbud and the dogwood, I visited the Wyaloosing, and walked down the deer path, and as I did, I talked to the deer and I talked to God. And suddenly I realized that something had lifted from me, the heavy weight of grief. Please understand, I still grieve, not acutely and not constantly, but one cannot lose a child without that lost being a significant part of one's life.

I finally saw 'her' not very long ago. She stepped out of the woods and raised her head and sniffed. She was lovely and graceful. She turned her head and looked my way. I stood stock still. Submerged in the shadows, I don't believe she saw me. Then she daintily stepped forward and made her way across the road and disappeared as she made her way down to the creek, the portion of the creek I foolishly call mine. No one owns a creek. For those of us who love the wooded places along the little creeks, we find that the creek comes to own us.

At the time of Clay's death, I was spending several days a week with my friend, Evelyn. Her husband, Herb had suffered a stroke and she needed help. When I was a teenager, I had been her 'girl'. She had three robust sons and no girls. Her hubby decided she needed a girl and suggested me. I become her Saturday girl and in the summers, went two or three days a week. I should have been paying her. She taught me how to iron properly, clean effectively, and make pickles, and she surrounded me with her gentle spirit and laughter and her wit and wisdom. Her boys were pretty much grown by this time, all a little older than me. One was in the Air Force when I started working for her, the middle one ignored me and the one closer to my age talked to me sometime. Danny also got in on the Beesley work crew. He mowed for Evelyn and later helped at haying time. We both have fond memories of our time spent on their farm. It was Herb, as a foreman at Cummins, who helped get Danny on after he finished high school. After an army stint, Danny returned to Cummins, and retired from Cummins in his fifties and went back to cutting grass (started a lawn care business).

I actually worked for Evelyn in three periods, as a teen and then during her husband's illness in the nineties and then after I retired when she herself was suffering from Parkinson and Dementia. By that time, her middle son had learned to talk and could only be outtalked by his older brother. Daughter-in-laws came in to help as well and I felt again a part of their large caring family. With her death in 2009, I lost the first of the many mothers I had collected, and there has been one a year since. It hurts, but I would not trade one moment of the time I spent with them. It is a great blessing to have one mother, and a greater blessing to have seven.

I haven't said much about Mom, who is Nora Elizabeth Detamore Reynolds Westover Neal Ernstes. That is because she is still alive and she is going to read this. It is much easier to write about someone who is gone. They can't correct you. But Mom was an over comer in her own way. She had a severe reading problem as a child, a disorder we now label dyslexia. She finally learned to read at eighteen and sign her name but has remained a poor speller. She actually loves to read and at eighty-seven is reading larger, more complex words than she ever has. There is so much we still don't know about how humans learn. Another strike against her had to do with her being the only girl in a group of three boys, and a girl raised largely by her father while her mother spent most of her life in the Richmond State Hospital with the old diagnosis of manic depressive syndrome. My grandmother should never have had children, and she had eight, four by her first husband and four with my grandfather. I remember her clearly even though I only got to visit with her about three times. Once was on the grounds of the state hospital. She was always drifty except once. On the last visit we had with her, she looked directly at me and told me to be a good girl. I was seventeen or eighteen at the time. Because of her condition, my mother and I and my children have tried to ward off our own depression and fight the sometimes tendency to move in that direction. I believe the condition is genetic but triggered by environmental influences and sometimes, with enough support, can be avoided. Not everyone agrees with me and that is all right. I hurt for my grandmother whom, I believe, was basically a good woman who loved her children, but could not function as a wife and mother in our society. Her family did not understand her and society rejected her. It was a time more than now that mental illness was considered something for a family to be ashamed of. I hope more people are looking at it as I do. It is an illness and should be treated as such, with persons getting the treatment they need as they would if diabetic or suffering from heart problems.

But as there were strikes against Mom, there were rooters on the sidelines. She had two loving aunts, Aunt Pete and Aunt Mary, who lived in the same neighborhood and helped raise my mom and her brothers as well as their own families. Her uncles were caring men who also lived nearby. As she got older, her older brother, Bill, took over much of the mother role in the family, doing the shopping and most of the cooking, and being protective of her. And even though in typical brother/sister fashion, she fought with her younger brother, they grew close as the years passed, and he took, too, took on a protective role. It took longer for her to realize that all her brothers loved her and wanted the best for her. In school, most of her teachers were patient with her, just unaware as to how to help her learn. Then there was a host of cousins and friends. But there is no question that a child with a severe learning disability has a tough time of it and their self esteem is seriously affected. Mom has had a long struggle, not only to learn, but to feel good about herself. Because of her struggle, I have not taken for granted my own ability to read and organize or my way with words. I am so thankful to have been given this gift, and I hurt for those who struggle with the written word. It is one of the reasons I wanted to teach. I am convinced that every person can learn if provided with the right tools at the time of their life when their mind is ready. My mother has never stopped learning. She learned to drive in her forties and to write out a check in her eighties, but those are big accomplishments for someone with her disability.

She was a very loving and affectionate mother. She gave hugs and kisses frequently and she sang with us (Old Dan Tucker and You got the money, Honey) and played games. She let us help in the kitchen although she was not a very good cook. I told her once as an adult, "Mom, that was great how you involved us in making hot chocolate, by mashing all the sugar and cocoa lumps and then mixing it all together. We thought it was necessary." She looked dumbfounded. "I thought it was," she replied. We also played games as a family, especially the card game, "Rummy". And sometimes on the way home from town on a Saturday night, we would all sing together, songs such as 'Froggie went a Courting' and 'My Bonnie Lies Over the Ocean' and 'Put on Your Old Gray Bonnet', and of course, 'Old Shep'. Rarer were outside games, but occasionally Dad or Mom would join us and the neighbor kids in a game of ball. Those are good memories.

Both parents gave us the gift of uncles and aunts. My dad's are mentioned here and there in this story because most of them were in Jennings

County. But I want to make special mention of my mother's siblings, especially her three full brothers. I have talked about her relationship with them, but not ours. They all lived in Marion where Mom grew up and that is where they raised their families. The usual visit schedule was our going to Marion for Mom's reunion held in August. We would stay at least the weekend as a rule and spent the night with one uncle or the other. Uncle Bill and Uncle Raggs lived in Bucktown, the area of Marion where Mom and her brothers had grown up, in the shadow of the Malleable, a foundry taking up an entire block. Uncle Lefty lived across town. Their visit schedule to see us in Jennings was more sporadic. It might be once a year and it might be the three of them (sometimes they would come at Christmas and take us shopping) (Also, if it was a work project they often came together-they helped Dad finish the house) or they may come with their families; Uncle Bill usually stopped on their way to Kentucky to see his wife's folks. They would stop at Scipio and get bologna and bread and we'd have lunch together and catch up, then they'd be on their way. It was Uncle Raggs and his family who sometimes spent the night. Uncle Raggs would arrive and after the all around hugs, he would bellow, "Where is that battery acid of your Dad's?" That was his referral to Dad's coffee. Dad boiled his coffee, leaving in the grounds. Uncle Raggs' girls', Debbie and Phyllis, loved going to the chicken house and gathering eggs. His girls were several years younger than Danny and me. Those visits provided a bonding time, and I will tell you that I knew I was loved by my uncles. I remember sharing special moments like dancing on Uncle Bill's feet and stretched out on the living room floor with him watching 'Have Gun, Will Travel'. With Uncle Raggs, my first bonding time came when I was about eighteen months old. He was home on leave (army) for the first time since my birth and most of the family had gathered at Aunt Pete's to share a meal and spend some time with him. Cousin Lenora, Aunt Pete's daughter, had made a chocolate cake, and to make up with me, Uncle Raggs sat and fed me that chocolate cake. I ate lots and amazingly did not get sick. There were lots of other special times, conversations and walks and drives. They were great uncles and they were greatly loved!

Mom also had three half sisters and one half brother. I never felt as close to them, partly because we did not spend as much time together (two sisters lived in California and one in Michigan) and partly because Uncle Highly died when I was still in my teens, but I knew they were my family and except for Aunt Mary Ann, whom I never met, I have some fond memories. My favorite memory with Aunt Lillian happened there on the Wyaloosing. Uncle Raggs had brought her down, at her request, to see us. (She was visiting Marion at the time.). She was very elegant looking, dressed fashionable. She asked to use the bathroom and it was I who escorted her to the old grey outside toilet facility and guarded the door. She took it all in with a laugh and I don't think either of us was embarrassed. For me, it was simply the way we lived, and for her, it had been a long, long time since she had lived that way. That was the sixties. Her last visit was in the nineties and she and we knew it would be her last. She was weepy as we parted. My uncles and aunts were all hard workers sharing a serious work ethic and a commitment to family'.

Those aunts and uncles left us with fourteen cousins. It was Billie that I was close to growing up. She and I were just four months apart and she was the oldest of Uncle Bill's three girls. When I spent the night with her in Marion, I had trouble falling asleep because I wasn't used to cars passing along the street. When she spent the night with me, she had trouble sleeping because she wasn't used to those noisy insects humming away or the lovely song of the Whipper-o-will. Billie was one of those many children who contracted polio in the forties, but she has never let that define her. She has lived a normal life with a teaching career and is the mother of four children and the wife of a grateful husband.

Our nearest neighbors both times we lived on the Wyaloosing were The Pettys. The Petty kids were in our age range, one slightly younger and three slightly older. They taught us to swim the summer we moved back to the Creek. Yes, in the creek with the crawdads and fish and snakes. That is where country children swam. We also skated on the backwater ice in winter, all wrapped up in our non matched coats and hats and scarves, country kids laughing and whooping it up. Sometimes I stand on the creek bank and I can see us. They were good friends and I've lost track of them. Both parents are gone now. Both were legally blind, and I was always amazed at what they could do.

There were three rental houses on our stretch of road and so some neighbors changed frequently but the ones that left an impact on our lives were the Cross family, and the Brooks family. Again they had children in our age range, but the Cross family kept having children so some are quite a bit younger than Danny and me. It was their oldest daughter, Irene, who was our baby sitter for a while.

Both Bessie Brooks and Lyda Cross were southern gals who made terrific baking powder biscuits. I loved accidently getting to their house at mealtime. They both patiently tried to teach me how to make those biscuits, but even though my yeast rolls are something to die for, I have never made a light, fluffy biscuit. Bessie was great about clearing their big kitchen table and making room for board games on snow days. One daughter was my age and a boy was Danny's age with two boys slightly younger but old enough to play board games with us. The last two of their children were cute little girls and were really my favorites. Some still live in the area and some are out of state.

It was coming back from their house one day in summer that Danny decided to do a bike stunt. It was simple and only dangerous because of the loose gravel on the road way. He would race up one of the logging roads into the woods and then race down the hill into the road. I warned him of the danger and tried to get him to stop, but obviously he was having too much fun. Then it happened! Riding like the wind, hair whipping around his face, he came flying down the hill, hit the loose gravel and down he went. I half carried him, half drug him the rest of the way home. He had a deep gash in his forehead and would have bruises in other places. At home, I cleaned the cut as much as I could. When our parents came home, Daddy cleaned it again and put a poultice on it and bandaged it. Mom wanted to take Danny to the doctor for stitches. But in our household, Dad ruled on such decisions. And a visit to the doctor was rare. However, Danny's cut began to look really bad, and Mom then enlisted Aunt Elizabeth to convince dad to take him to the doctor. Auntie could get him to do things where others failed. Finally, at the doctor, Dad was gently reprimanded by the doctor. The cut should have had stitches, but now it was too late, but the doctor did treat the gash. My dad was quite upset with himself. His treatment may have worked if it had not been a hot, sticky summer.

And he would have never deliberately put Danny in danger. The next year, he was the one who finally realized that Danny's tummy ache was more serious than the usual 24 hour bug. It was the last day of school, and Danny had not missed a day of the sixth grade so he told no one at first that his tummy hurt. He rode to school, got his certificate and rode the school bus back home. By then he was hurting more and spent the afternoon on the couch. Still not terribly concerned, Mom and I went to a graduation exercise that night with a neighbor. During that time, Dad decided that Danny's pain was not normal and took him to a neighbor and together, they took Danny to the hospital. Within an hour of arrival, Danny was in surgery, a simple appendectomy, but it had been a close call. Danny's appendix was about to burst. So even though Danny wasn't born in the Seymour Hospital, he did get a short stay there.

We were poor so it was rare for us to eat out, but one evening Dad told us we could go with him to Indianapolis for a fertilizer run. Oh boy, were we excited. The next morning we were up early and crawled into the old Chevy and went to work with Dad. At the sawmill, he scooted us up into the log truck (no seat belts) and off we went, to the far way city of Indianapolis. Of course, I am being sarcastic, but then it seemed far away and a little mystical. There was no interstate then. We drove up 31 and, perched high in the truck, viewed the world as new and undiscovered. At the stockyards, Dad expertly backed up the truck to a loading ramp, got out his little paper that stated how much fertilizer Uncle Archie wanted and took it up to the loading foreman. Within minutes, black men, shiny with sweat, muscles rippling, were loading sacks of fertilizer onto the truck. I had never seen black men at work, and was fascinated. In the background was the noise of the stockyards, pigs squealing and the lowing of unhappy cows. With our mission accomplished, Dad pulled smoothly out of the area and we were soon back on 31 headed home. About half way home, Dad asked if we would like a hamburger. Of course, we said 'yes'. Dad stopped at a roadside restaurant (or more commonly referred to as a hamburger joint) and going in, picked us up and plopped us on stools, and ordered for us and himself. It surely was the best hamburger I had ever eaten, because it was a rare treat. It was and still is one of the very favorite memories of my childhood. There were other times we went with Dad on the log truck, and those were times we actually stood and watched as he loaded logs with a winch. Another fun thing about being the children of a sawmill man was getting to play in the sawdust piles (of course, this was only at times the mill was completely shut down).

And of course, our dad was the one who took us to the creek for our first fishing experience. I noticed the other day as I drove by the creek how that little sandbar we first fished on had grown. And I was called back in time to being a ten year old with an old cane pole and a can of slimy worms and a sunny day and sharing a new experience with my dad and brother. I honestly can't remember if I caught a fish or not. That really wasn't the most important object of the time. You have to be in a child's life today if you want to be in his memory tomorrow.

I know this has been a collage of stories but this short autobiography of Danny and my lives is not suppose to be complete but sketchy at best. It is written for our grandchildren, to give them some idea what our growing up, formative years were like and how important that little stretch of land is that clings to the Wyaloosing. All has been sold but a mere two acres that I have kept with our camping spot. I will keep that as long as I can and walk those trails until I am not able to do so anymore which will probably be soon. But always I will remember the discovery of Dutchman Breeches in the early spring and the spring beauties and wood violets, the unfurling of tiny green leaves, the many songs the Wyaloosing sings, roaring at flood time, musical at her best, sometimes gurgling, especially over rocks, and there are times there is no music. The creek goes dry or at least in sections. In the fall, all of Jennings County is covered with a riotous array of color but I love to stand in the woods and smell fall and if I listen quietly, sometimes I am rewarded with the bark of a squirrel nearby or the chirp of a chipmunk or the plunking sound as a black walnut or buckeye hits the ground or the almost silent flutter of a leaf. In winter, I still walk. There is a special winter silence in the woods.

It was my dream to come back and build a cabin on the Wyaloosing and live my life out there, but some dreams have to be forfeited. Nearby, my Uncle Archie spent his last days on the Wimple as he wanted with my beloved Aunt Elizabeth, my father's sister, at his side, but the time

came when we were no longer able to care for her in the house he had
built her in the forties and which he and she had made a home, not only
welcoming and nourishing their children, but their grandchildren and
great grandchildren and their nieces and nephews. He gave me my first
Bible, told me to read it everyday. She taught me how to bake angel food
cake and yeast rolls and she tried to teach me how to sew. How many
times did she say, "Can't you keep that seam straight?" She gave me my
first perm and laughed as Uncle Archie came in holding his nose. It
was he that was the other man I called the night my daddy died. Uncle
Archie was daddy's brother-in-law, his employer and his friend. Uncle
Archie and Aunt Elizabeth loved their garden and although always
generous with us, they were frugal people. The summer before he died,
I stopped at their place on my way to Columbus to visit my brother's
family. They were sitting under a tree shelling peas. Aunt Elizabeth
had asked several people to pull the pea vines including me and no one
had gotten around to it, so she did it herself, and now her back was
killing her. Did I feel guilty or what? I tried to redeem myself by sitting
down and helping shell peas. Uncle Archie was shirtless on that warm
summer day but in his bib overalls which was his dress of choice. After
a good chat, Aunt Elizabeth made me feel even guiltier by insisting I
take some peas up to my brother (my brother's family hated peas). I
insisted that I not, but as usual, she won. She got up with a moan and
went into the house to get a sack. I looked at Uncle Archie and said,
"What a stubborn woman!" And he looked intently at me and replied,
"Not a bit more than me." They were married almost sixty years. Their
lives together were good, but they had their heartaches, including the
loss of two daughters, one in infancy and one at age twenty-two in an
automobile accident, killed instantly by a drunken driver. Karen and
her husband had just driven safely all the way from California where
Karen's husband had just been released from his military obligation.
What irony! They had a two year old son who had been left home with
the family as they went for a Sunday afternoon drive to look at trailers.
They took along Karen's sister, Patty and her husband, who were in the
back seat and suffered serious injuries as did Karen's husband. I was
stricken when I heard the news. I had gone to the church for a youth
program and everyone was talking about it. I rushed back home to my
dad. Karen was his favorite niece. It was one of the few times I saw
him cry. He never wore a tie, but for Karen, he went out and bought

a red tie for her funeral. Thirty some years later, my son, at the same age would die in an accident, and my aunt would reach back into those days of pain in order to share my grief. One night when she was nearly ninety, I stopped at her house after fighting my way toward home in an almost blinding snow storm from New Castle where I was working at the time. I gasped as she opened the door, "I just can't go any farther." I was only seven miles from my house in North Vernon. She put me on the couch, covered me with a blanket and made me a hot cup of tea. I stayed the night, not an unusual occurrence. She was a giver and I loved her. What else can I say? Perfect? Hardly! But she loved! All I can hope is someone will say the same thing about me.

Their house still stands along State Road 3 and on Wimple Creek. The sawmill is crumbling but the mill pond is still there. On the other side of the Highway there is no sign of the Wimple school house that once set there and few remember it, but I know Uncle Archie attended there because he told me so. The brick building blew up in 1949. (a gas explosion). It was being used as a house at the time, and Lucille (Tommie) Littell Jones grabbed her baby girl and ran for protection in the culvert. Her husband, Lester, (Leck) was in the barn milking and was thrown from his milk stool by the blast. The baby girl in this story is my dear friend, Charlotte. We shared Sunday School and church, school and a few girlhood over nighters.

In this biographical sketch, I could not possibly touch on all the people who have made a difference in my life, but the emphasis has been on those who shared our formative years. The other sketches in this book have to be considered fiction because I have added flesh to the bare facts I have about my ancestors. In these sketches, fact and fiction are combined but the facts are shown to be such, so that if you are a researcher, you will have some idea of my sources. This sketch, however, is as true as my memory serves. (Loralyn Reynolds, 2014)

A Snowy Day

I love the snow
God knows
Especially
When I'm inside
All snug and warm.

I can enjoy its beauty
Lace covered bushes
Snow covered roofs
Safely inside
Beside the fireside.

Yet I sometimes long
To be outside
And go a good tromp
Through the white snow
But, lo, I am old!
(A Snowy Day, January 21, 2014)

Loralyn Reynolds

Where the Wyaloosing Flows

Where the Wyaloosing flows
I will grow old
Like my father
Before me
And others
Of family lore

Well, at least
That's how I had it planned.

But some things don't go
The way that we intend.
And dreams have to give way
To life's stringent demands.

Before I grew old,
Really old,
Parkinson Disease stole my body
But not my soul.

No, not my soul
Never my soul.
It belongs to the Wyaloosing
And it belongs to God!

Along the Banks of the Wyaloosing

1853 to 1940s

The Story of the Renn Family

HN: Henry and Rachel Renn, my great, great, great grandparents were the first of my ancestors to settle on the Wyaloosing. They did so in 1853. I researched land records to confirm this. They came from Pennsylvania per census records and Aunt Edith. I have confirmed Rachel's parents, Robert and Elizabeth Campbell, and her sister, Anna Elizabeth, who married Daniel Mowery. (The library at North Vernon has a book on the Daniel Mowery family. They also have the Renn Family History which is more extensive than my work here.) By 1843, the Mowery's, too, were in Decatur County. I cannot determine for sure who Henry's parents were or go farther back than Robert Campbell. The best guess for Robert's (who was born in New Jersey in 1774) is Daniel Campbell who had a son Robert of about that age. This comes from a history of Northumberland County, PA by Herbert C. Bell. The best guess for Henry is Henry or John Henry. The following story is considered fiction but all names and dates are confirmed by census records, marriage records and older family members.

The Man from Pennsylvania

"Yah". Henry Renn called to his horses, slapped the reins over their gray backs, and the heavily loaded wagon pulled away from their Pennsylvania cabin. Rachel sat on the seat beside the lanky man who had been her husband for sixteen years. She held the baby, Isabel, on her lap. She did not look back. One does not look back unless that is the direction they are headed.

The four older children, including Susanna, fifteen, Alex who was eight, Enoch at six and Isaac at four, laughingly ran along the wagon. They would soon tire and each would take their turns in the wagon, especially

Isaac. The year was 1838. Henry's father had died months ago and with him all ties to Pennsylvania. Behind the cabin they had left were four graves, his parents and two children they had lost. Rachel's parents', Robert and Elizabeth Campbell, had taken their youngest three sons and left for Indiana several years before. Now Elizabeth had written urging her oldest daughter and family to come. Robert was not well, and she wanted all her family near.

It had not been an easy decision, but game was getting scarce, and Henry was not much of a farmer, but a hunter of game. He knew how to build a cabin, wield an axe, dig a well, and put in a little corn, but he provided for his family mainly by the long rifle that rode by his side.

They made their first river crossing that day, the first of many. This was the mighty Susquehanna. Both he and Rachel had been born in this mountainous area of middle Pennsylvania. Their neighbors included German and Scotch Irish settlers. The Scotch Irish were especially 'a moving on' kind of people, as indicated by Rachel's dad. Robert Campbell had been born in New Jersey, moved to Pennsylvania where most of his children were born and then moved as an old man to Indiana. Henry thought Robert also fit the profile of the typical Scotch Irish male-proud, stubborn, tenacious.

I will not describe all the rivers and creeks they crossed or how many snakes surprised them. They did get to Indiana with minor complaints, sunburn and bug bites and poison ivy, scratches and cuts, loss of a calf and loss of a prized rose bush. Rachel mourned that loss the most. She had dug it up herself and carefully wrapped it for the journey. Such a fragrant rose!

Arriving in Decatur County at the Campbell farm, they found Robert worse than when the letter had come. Elizabeth was worn to a frazzle. Elizabeth was overjoyed to see them but five children added to a household is always a big challenge. Rachel gave birth to a daughter, Sarah, the next year and they made plans to buy a piece of land from Robert and build their own house which they did in 1842.

But Henry was not satisfied. For one thing, he missed the hills. Jackson Township in Decatur County was flat as a flitter. SO he kept his eye out, especially when hunting game took him for miles. One day, while following a deer, he found it! It was a stretch of land like back home, a hilly farm with a creek, a pretty creek called 'The Wyaloosing'. In 1853, he sold his Decatur holdings and bought twenty acres from the Howe's and moved his family, including Elizabeth, (Robert had died around 1845-46) to the farm on the Wyaloosing. He soon added to the cabin that was on the place and put out his first corn. He also dug a well. He chose a site by devining and found good water. He dug down as far as he could and then tied a rope around his small son and Will's little friend (taking turns) and lowered them into the well. The boys dug for a short time and he would haul them back up. Will did not mind the darkness as the well got deeper because he had been born blind. His friend gave out though but helped Henry inbed creek stones into the walls of the well. Besides Will, Henry and Rachel had another child before Rachel reached the time of life when child bearing was over. She was forty-two when Mary Ellen was born.

HN: But if Henry and Rachel thought their family was complete, they were wrong. In 1862, their son Isaac, who worked for the railroad, brought home to them his three day old son, placed the infant in his mother's arms and said, "I have a gift for you'. The baby's mother had died in childbirth. SO John Henry Renn was raised by his grandparents on the Wyaloosing and he must have felt the love for the creek and place as would my father years later. Even though he lost the acreage his grandfather gave him when he was young, he came back years later (1910) and bought the Cadby farm down the road and south on the creek from the original Renn holdings. At John Henry's death, the house and land went to his son and later in a divorce settlement to his daughter in law who happened to be a cousin, the warm, loving and rather unpredictable Cora Renn, who was the granddaughter of Sarah Renn Howe, raised by her grandmother whose house was just across the road from the Cadby house and just down from the Pleasant View Church. The original Renn holdings include land on the right going north on State Road 3 where the Wyaloosing crosses under the road. Henry bought forty more acres the year of 1853, and forty more later, all adjoining the original twenty.

Cora Renn was a gracious lady, played the piano at Pleasant View for revivals, took in her first cousin, Roy Hockersmith, who was a bit slow and watched after him, and helped her kin when things were tough. She also provided a place of refreshment during the prohibition for interested patrons and sometimes, it is said, the patrons brought ladies with them. I remember her dimly as a child but I find her inconsistencies interesting and am somewhat fascinated by her. I believe I will see her in heaven someday.

She lived on the farm on the Wyaloosing through the depression and into the forties, the only Renn descendent I know that lived on the Wyaloosing into that decade; then we came in 1947. It is like, maybe, destiny. The creek has a claim on our family.

Now I need to skip back to Henry and Rachel's children. I am not going into great detail except for my family line which is Enoch, since there is a book in the library on Renn history, listing scads of relatives. But I will give a brief summary.

Their oldest daughter, Susannah, married William Herron in 1843 in Decatur County. In 1850 they still lived in Decatur and had four children. In 1860, they were in Shelby County with four more children. IN 1870, they are found in Bartholomew County and surprise, they have three more children. It was their son, James, who ends up marrying his first cousin, Etta, Mary Ellen" daughter. Alex or Alexander married Sarah Jane Cooper in 1849. She died in childbirth. He then married Eliza Ann Skiles. Their daughter, Charity, married Sylvanus Thurston, brother of Rebecca Thurston who married Enoch Renn. They ended up being the grandparents of Joy Thurston. When I met Joy, she was a retired teacher who was also researching these families. She had two sisters, one married to a Gregory. You've already heard about Isaac, but he did remarry, a Sarah Jane Sanders and had another son, Joseph. Losing this wife, also, he married Mary Lewellan. His son, John Henry, who was raised by Rachel and Henry, had five children. It is John Henry's granddaughter, Mardella Elmore, who researched and wrote an extensive family history for the Renn family and gave me a lot of verbal history. Her aunt Elizabeth, or 'Betty' Archer wrote to me and sent me helpful information on the family.

Isabella is next. In 1854, she married James Bias who was a Civil War Veteran (CO. I, 38th Indiana Volunteers) and they lived on a farm on what is now Base road a few short miles out of Brewersville. There were seven children. In the history of the Pleasant View Church, James is mentioned. I can only assume that others of his family and some of the Renn family attended the church. At that time, it was a United Brethren Church. Isabel's daughter, Phoebe Jane, married Isaac Hooten and Phoebe and Isaac bought forty acres from Henry in 1883. (In 2014, this farm belongs to Bryan Chaille). James died in 1898 and is buried at Cave Springs. (So is one of his grandchildren who died in his teens). Many of the Renn descendents are buried there.

Sarah is the first child to have been born in Indiana. She married George Howe whose parents sold Henry his first twenty acres in Jennings County. She ended up living her days out in an old house on the twenty acres of Howe land that wasn't sold to Henry. This was just up from the Pleasant View Church on a stretch of State Road 3. She had two daughters, and helped raise both of their children, Cora Smith Renn and Roy Hockersmith. Both Cora and Roy are buried at Cave Springs. As a child, I walked in the cemetery many, many times and was so fascinated by the stories told by the stones. There is a row of children's graves that shows three children of the same family died within weeks of each other, probably a fever that spread through the community or a fire. But how heartbreaking! It is hard enough to lose one child. I know. But to lose three at the same time? However, as I wondered about the stories of the stones, I had no idea that I had as many relatives buried among them. Eli Thurston and his wife are there as well as his sons, James Luther and Charles. Then up to twenty Renn cousins.

Now Will or William. He married Charlotte Hoggersmith (?) in 1865 and farmed near his dad. Will died in 1909. There is no record of children.

Now Mary Ellen. I will write a little more about her for three reasons. One she was the baby and stayed on the farm with Henry until his death and afterwards. Two, she seems to have been a favorite of her brother, Enoch. He named a daughter after her. And three, she has descendents still in this area.

Ellen or Mary Ellen married Frank Hartwell. He died in 1885, found frozen to death on his way home. He had been drinking. Her three children at the time were still in their teens. They all married rather early, probably because of the situation. Ellen remarried in 1887, to Isaac Towne, shortly after Henry's death. Henry died because he had gotten his feet frozen while doing chores. He was around eighty-five years old. They took him back to the Mowery Cemetery in Decatur County to be laid beside Rachel. Also buried there are Rachel's parents, Robert and Elizabeth Campbell and her sister and husband, Daniel and Elizabeth Anna Mowery. The Cemetery is near the little town of Alert. One must cross a farmer's field to get to it. It is on land that Robert Campbell once owned. Later it was owned by his sons, but sold before 1900.

Mary Ellen had a rough time, I am sure, with her husband and father's deaths so close together. It is no wonder she allowed Etta to marry at fourteen, and to her first cousin, James Herron, whom she had always loved. Ellen's'daughter, Susan, had married David Franks in 1885 shortly after the death of Frank Hartwell. David was fifteen years older than she. They remained in Sand Creek township and had seven children. He died in 1906 of heart disease at age fifty-three and is buried at Cave Springs with one of their children, Dessia, who died in 1909 at age four from accidental burns, a common enough tragedy in the days of fireplaces and wood burning stoves. Susan remarried in 1912.

Etta and James had seven children, losing two at a young age to pneumonia. By 1900, they were in Bartholomew County and were there in 1925 when Mary Ellen died. Etta's other children were Rachel, Esta Pearl, Amanda, Leonard, and Edward. I am going to include here the obituary of Flossie Palmer which I found in 2013. She is the daughter of Amanda Herron and John Thomas Wells and the only recent update I have found of any of the descendents of Etta Hartwell and James Herron.

Flossie A. Palmer, 92, is laid to rest at Columbus: Flossie A. "Nellie" Palmer, 92, of Columbus died at 4:25 a.m. Tuesday, May 21, 2013, at her home. Funeral services were Friday at Columbus First Assembly of God on 10th Street with Pastors Rick Glowacki and Donald P. Andreasen officiating. Burial will be at Garland Brook Cemetery in Columbus. Myers-Reed Chapel in Columbus was in charge of arrangements. Mrs. Palmer retired in 1988 from Cummins Engine Company and was a lifelong member of Columbus First Assembly of God. She enjoyed gardening, canning, traveling and reading her Bible. She loved spending time with her family. Born in Columbus April 15, 1921, Mrs Palmer was the daughter of Thomas and Amanda Herron Wells. She married John R. Palmer Nov. 21, 1947 in Columbus. He preceded her in death June 15, 1993. Survivors include daughters, Karen Hazley of Bellingham, Washington, Sadie (David) Cress and Trudy (Bill) Zimmerman, all of Columbus. Mandy Beier of Hope, Nancy Palmer and Vickie Garrett, of Scipio and Rhonda (James) Davis of Ohio; sons, Fred (Stella) Jackson of Oklahoma, Duain (Pamela) Palmer of North Vernon, Jerry Ray (Marsha) Palmer and Todd Palmer, both of Columbus; 36 grandchildren; several great and great-great grandchildren and several half brothers and sisters. Mrs. Palmer was preceded in death by her parents, her husband, daughters, Evelyn Eddleman and Patsy Barrix; sons, Chester Leroy Jackson and Larry Jay Palmer; two grandchildren; two sisters; one brother and four half-brothers and sisters.

Enoch Renn was the second son and third child of Rachel and Henry Renn. He was about six years old when they made the trip to Indiana so he should of have had memory of the trip. He was twenty-one years old when he married Rebecca Thurston. They married January 1, 1854 in Decatur County and were married by a minister, Daniel Griffin. Rebecca was only fourteen years old but turned fifteen in February. She may have married early because of her father's death. Sylvanus died in a farming accident in 1852 leaving Rebecca's mother with four children under the age of twelve. That would have been very difficult. Enoch and Rebecca may have met while she was being farmed out to a family living near Henry and Rachel. The year before, Henry had taken Rachel and his younger children to Jennings County. Or the families may have known each other back in Pennsylvania. They came from the same area, the names of Pottsville and Sunbury mentioned in both family histories. Anyway, census record find Enoch and Rebecca still in Decatur County in 1860 and their oldest daughter and my great grandmother was born there in November of 1854. The 1860 census also tells us that Enoch's sister, Sarah, and her husband, George Howe, were living with them. The two couples were about the same age. By 1870, we find Enoch and Rebecca in Jennings with a William Davis and they have another daughter, Elisha, living with them. There was almost eight years between the girls and it states several places that Rebecca gave birth to four children. We can only assume that two died at birth. In 1880, they have a John listed with them. It turns out he is not a son but a train orphan. In 1880, Enoch is listed as a Stationary Engineer. In 1900, we find Enoch and Rebecca alone and living on their small farm right outside Brewersville. In December of 1901, Enoch fell doing chores and broke his hip. He died December 31 and was buried in January in the Kellar Cemetery nearby. We can assume he was well loved. Newspaper listings of the time indicate that he was visited by at least three nephews at the time of his accident, Charles Thurston, (Rebecca's nephew), John Renn, or John Henry, Isaac's son, and Robert Herron, Susanna's son. Rebecca is still found on her little farm in 1910. She did whatever she needed to get by. She was a laundress for four years in a private home and made and sold quilts, kept a garden and chickens and smoked a pipe. She lived to be eighty-five years old and spent the last few years in Indianapolis probably with her daughter, Elisha who married a Coryell. She is buried near siblings, Sylvanus Thurston and Louisa Robbins in the North Vernon Cemetery, because her space beside Enoch had been taken by a grandchild. Rebecca's obituary indicates she was a woman of faith and a member of the Baptist Church. I have a picture of her but not of my great grandmother. I can only assume that Mary Ellen favored her mother and me, a short, plumpish woman, somewhere between pretty and plain.

If you have followed this story and I know it jumps around, you will know by now that Enoch and Rebecca Thurston Renn's daughter, Mary Ellen, is the mother of my Grandfather Reynolds which makes her my great grandmother. She married Merritt Reynolds in 1877 and my grandfather, William Edwin Reynolds was born August of 1878 near Brewersville. If you wish to read more about Mary Ellen, it is included in the Reynolds section, The Reynolds Family on Sand Creek.

If you want more on Rebecca Thurston and the Thurston family, see the section on The Thurston Family on the Wyaloosing and Bear Creek.

Renn and Campbell Tidbits

Herein are some gleanings from my research that may be or may not be of interest to you.

Campbell Land Transactions:

William H Campbell from John Walker; Warrenty Deed; August 1839; $5.00; N part S18twp10Range18

Robert Campbell from James and Anne Lloyd; Warranty Deed; March 9, 1840; $1,050.00; NE Qtr; 5, 8, 8

Robert Campbell, JR from Robert Campbell, Sr. (Wife Elizabeth); Warranty April 26, 1845 Part NE Qtr 5, 8, 8; 12 acres.

William and Alex Campbell from Robert Campbell, SR; April 26, 1845; E ½ NE Qtr 5, 8, 8
SW Qtr of NE Qtr 5, 8, 8; 96 acres.

*The last two transactions were given in love and affection to the above, Robert Jr. named as a son and the other two implied, given for their support and maintenance.

Alex sold to Wm Belt in 1857.
Alex sold to Hannah Rodgers in 1859 5 acres in 5, 8, 8 for $100.00.
Alex sold to Overton Hearne 40 acres in 1882.

Robert Campbell to Henry Renn Jan 1842; $150.00; 40 acres; Not recorded until 1852.
Henry Renn to Isaac Skiles; NW Qtr of NE Qtr of Sec 5 Twp 8, N Range 8; 40 acres; $800.00; January 27, 1853.

Newspaper Gleanings

Civil War veteran James Bias, of Sand Creek township, served in NC; 38 Reg.

Loralyn Reynolds

(was husband of Isabella Renn)

William Campbell, died at Westport 1886, burial at Campbell's Grove.

Carl Bious, born 1890, died January 14, 1905, son of George Bias and Alice Day, g-son of J. Bias & Isabella Renn, Rheumatic Fever' burial Cave Springs.

Children of Elisha Renn and Malcomb Coryell (this is the other daughter of Enoch Renn)

Emma born 1882; Emerson (died young)
Cecilia born 1888; Harold born 1895
Claudia born 1898 and Mary born 1900

When the Wyaloosing Sings

I love to hear the Wyaloosing sing
In the summer, winter and in the spring!
She is a little stream
But gladness
To my heart she brings.

In 1950
My dad bought a little piece of land
Built there a house with his own hands
I guess in my eyes
No one has ever measured up
To such a man!

Now when I reflect the years
I have loved this land'
And watched the Wyaloosing
At every stage:
Dry as a bone or
Wailing with rage,
And all the phases in between,
Murmuring gaily over rocks and sand
Happy with itself and the land.

To this place I come again and again,
Here I seek God,
And find Him
Among the wildflowers of Spring
The summer bird song
The flaming colors of fall
And the winter stillness.

Here I played as a child
Grew to womanhood, Somewhat.

Brought my children
And my children's children
To skip rocks
Wade in the creek
Fish on a summer day
Identify bird song and wildflowers
Hike, camp and find special rocks.
Watched Darby baptized
Beneath the Sentinel's spreading arms
Dealt with tearing grief
And found peace!

Along the Banks of the Wyaloosing-1860s to 1990s-the Story of the Thurston-Clarkson Family

My Uncle Eli

Somewhere near a rooster crowed, breaking the morning silence. The day was dawning clear and the slightly stooped older man was walking slowly as he saw to the various morning chores. He enjoyed the early morning and the quiet. Even the sound of the chickens clucking around his feet seemed to blend into the morning stillness. He had been feeding chickens and gathering eggs for many a morning. On one nest, a hen refused to move and he considered her and decided to let her remain. If she was in the mood for biddies, it may be well. He glanced down at the number of eggs in the basket, and knew they would be sufficient for the day's needs with a few, perhaps, left for selling. Like most men, he let his wife keep the egg and butter money. A woman needed a little money of her own. He had a good wife. He had been a most blessed man. He would never be rich or even well off, but he had kept a roof over their head and food on the table. The little farm here on the Wyaloosing had provided. He had bought it soon after he had come back from the war, a war that should never have happened, and he had suffered all these years from the effects of the three years he had been part of the northern army. He had willingly gone, a boy of eighteen, but was so glad neither of his sons had had to go to war. War is no place for a boy to become a man. And thousands of boys had gone to war, become men on those battlefields and never come back. Oh well, he mused, it was too lovely a morning for such thoughts. Like most men who had gone to war and come back, he did not like to talk about those days. They were not days that he wanted to remember. What he wanted to remember was the laughter of his children and grandchildren as they had played here on this land and in these woods and swam in the creek. He had expected more grandchildren, but Charles did not seemed inclined to marry and James Luther and his wife, Mary, had lost their only child and could not have more. His daughter, Etta, had tried to make up for her brothers, it seemed, but had stopped at seven. He loved them all but was especially fond of little Georgie. If George had spent the night, he would have been up gathering eggs with his grandfather.

Eli took his eggs and made his way back to the house. Leaving the basket in its usual place, he ventured out of doors again, making his way to the barn. Charles would soon be out to help. He pushed aside the thoughts that he didn't want to deal with such as what would happen to the farm when he was gone. Would Charles keep it up? No, he must not worry over what he could not control. He had done his best with his children. If Charles wasn't the farmer he had hoped he would be, he would do. James was the more diligent worker. Well, no one knows the outcome when a man and woman come together. He hoped he might have made his own dad proud. He would never know. His own father had died when he was a little boy, from a senseless farm accident. It had been really hard on his mother to finish raising her children, the oldest barely in her teens. Poor Becky, she had married at fourteen with her mother's encouragement. He was sure his mother felt there was not much choice. He still remembered how much he had missed Becky when she had left. She had been a second mother to him. She lived at Brewersville now and sometimes he would stop, especially if he had something to share like sausage after a butchering or a mess of fish. He did delight in taking a few hours and a grandchild by the hand and going to the creek. The creek offered bluegill and crappie and sometimes a nice bass. Nothing better than a pan of crisply fried fresh fish. Yes, he reflected, he had had a good life. And if it was soon coming to an end, so be it. He was ready for whatever lay on the other side. His body would rest in the small cemetery nearby but he was confident his soul and his spirit would be in another place, a place where he would feel the peace he was feeling now, forever.

HN: I never met the man yet I know him, I do. I've studied his life and loved his grandchildren and great grandchildren and I think I would have liked him and would have enjoyed walking beside him as he went about his chores, milking cows, and gathering eggs on his little farm on be banks of the Wysloosing. He bought his farm (Section 32, Geneva township) in the 1870s when he came back from the war, that is the Civil War (Company K, 82nd Indiana Volunteer Infantry, mustered in at Tripton, old name for North Vernon, on August 30, 1862). He married the girl he loved, Louisa Jane Shields (Lizzie), daughter of William Shields and Matilda Brinker. Lizzie was born March 4, 1846, Eli January 7, in 1844. They raised their family on the farm on the Wyaloosing and Rattail (a smaller creek nearby that empties into the Wyaloosing. That family included three children, James Luther, born 1869, who married Mary Stewart November of 1897 and whose only child died in infancy. Luther and Mary were married in her parents' home. Eli second child was Charles, born 1872 and who never married and Eli's daughter, Etta, born 1874, who married George Clarkson and had seven children, giving Eli his only living descendants. She made up for her brothers, with most of her children and children's children continuing to live in Jennnings County or nearby Decatur or Bartholomew counties. Following is a list of those I know.

Eli died in April of 1912; wife not until 1927. Charles continued to live on the farm until his death in 1946. (Note again that Mom and Dad brought me to the Wyaloosing in 1947). The land stayed in the family, tied up in court for too many years until it was all finally resolved and sold. Uncle Eli is buried with most of his immediate family in the Cave Springs Cemetery.

Now why is this mild mannered man so important to me?? Surely not his looks. He was five foot and nine inches with black hair and blue eyes, slightly built but strong in his youth. And not that he fought in a war even though I am proud to know he did and sorry that he suffered his entire adult life as a result of that experience. No, the importance of his life rests in that he was the brother of my great-great grandmother, Rebecca Thurston Renn. She was born in Pennsylvania in 1839 and came with her parents, Sylvanus and Lucinda Beers Thurston, to Indiana by covered wagon stopping in Ripley County to allow Eli to be born there. Another daughter, Louisa, was born in 1848 and a son, Sylvanus Weldon, was born in Jennings in 1850. In 1852, Sylvanus died in a farming accident on Devils' Ridge which is on Bear Creek. They buried him in a small farm cemetery which was on land owned by Grizzard family, the French Cemetery. Lucinda was left with four children under twelve years of age. Probably from necessity she married James Clark in 1855, but in the meantime, allowed Rebecca to marry

Enoch Renn in 1854. (Rebecca's story continues with the Renn and Reynolds sections).

Sylvanus Thurston came from a long line of big families which we can trace to the boarding of a ship, the Mary Anne, in 1637 by carpenter, John Thurston and his wife, Margaret, and their two sons, John and Thomas. They sailed from England. Both were from Wrentham in Suffolk. The Thurston name is associated with fine furniture in England and Scotland, the furniture that graces the houses of kings. In 1643, John and Margaret were in Medfield, Massachusetts. In 1640 twin sons were born, Joseph, who is our direct ancestor, and Benjamin. Several generations later another direct ancestor, Moses Thurston, of Ruston, Pennsylvania, sired a son in 1810, named Sylvanus, who in our Sylvanus. Indications of documentation show the family to be quite close knit. There were Thurston cousins already living in Jennings County when Sylvanus came. We know that Moses was a weaver by trade.

Lucinda was the daughter of Eli and Susan Beers. Beers is a Dutch name. Louisa, Rebecca's sister, married Joseph Robbins in 1868. She had two children, one was a daughter, Effie, (1873-1935) and Sanford (1869-1870)) and that is all the knowledge we have of her family. I don't think Effie ever married. Louisa and Joseph, Rebecca, and Sylvanus Weldon are all buried in the cemetery at North Vernon, in a row. Effie was a teacher.

Following is a Thurston history provided by Cousin George Thurston of Indianapolis. He copied it from a book on Thurston history, compiled by Brown Thurston, and sent it to Joy and I.

Brief Thurston Family History

John Thurston (1607 to 1685) of Wrentham, Suffolk, England, carpenter and freeman, age 30 and Margaret his wife, age 32, (1605-1662), and sons, Thomas, (born 1633) and John, (born 1635) left England on 10th of May 1637 on the Mary Anne of Yarmouth, Captain William Goose.

In 1643 they settled in Medfield, Massachusetts after a stay in Dedham. On the ship that brought them across were the following passengers of note: A Lace Poyett of Norwich, spinster, age 23. A JoAnes of Yarmouth, under 50 with Ruth and William and John.

This journey took place seventeen years after the Mayflower arrived.

Besides sons, John and Thomas, John and Margaret had six other children. Their son, Joseph, a twin was born in Dedham, on July 15, 1640. The other twin was Benjamin who married Elizabeth Walker. The twins were baptized the day of their birth. Other children were Mary, Daniel, Judith and Hannah. Joseph married a woman named Anne. He was a tax collector, had eight children and died about 1710. His son, Benjamin, married a woman named Sarah, had 3 children. Benjamin's son John was born February 28, 1703 and he married a Grace Olive Lucretia or perhaps that was more than one wife. Or did he marry Christina Pangburn. Maybe Israel married Christina Pangburn. The notes are confusing here. Anyway, John had ten children including Israel B, born December 6, 1734 (died 1790). Israel had six sons, Including Samuel, Benjamin, Moses and Flavel. Moses and Flavel are ancestors to the Jennings County Thurstons. Samuel was George Thurston's ancestor.

Moses was born May 9, 1770, married Catherine Bottenhomer and later Elizabeth Chester. He was a weaver and a Baptist in Rushton, PA and he died September 22, 1848. He had ten children, including Sylvanus B., our ancestor, who was born February 9, 1806 in Sunbury, Pennsylvania (Northumberland County) and married Lucinda Beers (1815-1878) in Pennsylvania. She was born in New Jersey or Connecticut.

As already mentioned, Sylvanus and Lucinda had four children, Rebecca who married Enoch Renn and parented our great-grandmother, Mary Ellen Renn Reynolds; Eli (1844-1912), who married Louisa Jane Shields and became the ancestor of 'the Clarkson clan'; Louisa Mariah, (1848-1922), who married Joseph C. Robbins and had two children, Sanford (only lived a year) and Effie who never married; and Sylvanus Weldon, (1851-1919) who became the ancestor of Joy Thurston and her sisters through his son, James. By his second marriage, seventeen years later, he had a daughter named Leona. Lucinda remarried, a James Clark, but in 1870 census she is listed alone in North Vernon and in 1880 census, she is in Sand Creek and daughter, Louisa Robbins and granddaughter Effie are living with her.

Israel's son Flavel, had a son named Moses who married Martha Willet and had a son, Samuel, who married Ann Brown and he owned a house in Brewersville in 1880s. A newspaper clipping of the time mentions the Thurston Brothers Mill, in fact, mention is made 1885, 1888 and 1889. Wish I knew more about it. I have been in contact with Charles Thurston who grew up in Jennings County. His line is Israel, Flavel, Jesse, Levi, Chester, then himself.

Israel's other sons we know little of. Samuel, born March 6, 1766 married Hannah Kelly. Another son, Benjamin, fought in the war of Revolution.

*included is a copy of an 1884 map showing Eli Thurston's farm

Descendants of Eli Thurston

❖ I am listing here the descendants of Eli Thurston that I know, for two reasons, one is that many live locally and two, many are personal friends. I have already listed the three children of Eli Thurston. Only one of those children produced offspring that lived to produce more offspring and that was their daughter, Etta, who married George Clarkson, and had several children. Eli's son, Charles never married, and his son, Luther James or James Luther had one child that died quite young. Luther and his wife were members of the Pleasant View Church. Perhaps so was Eli and Jane (Eli's funeral was held at Pleasant View Church) but we have documentation concerning Luther. Also they are remembered by Thelma Jones who was a child at the time that they were older members of the church.

On January 29, 1899, Etta married George Clarkson, who was a United Brethren minister, and usually assigned locally. George was the son of John and Harriet Perry Clarkson and George was born in 1870s. The seven children of George and Etta were Onita, John, Virgie, Chesley, Velma and George and?. Chesley's son, Russell, is the father of Thomas and Steve Clarkson who live locally. Thomas has two girls, Amanda and Rachel. Russell also had a daughter, Deanna Clarkson, who was living in Washington and has a daughter, Zoe Catsiff. George's family is listed next.

George William Clarkson was born March 11, 1913 in Jennings CO. He died January 2, 1970 at age 56. He is buried in the Vernon Cemetery. He married Juanita Olive Buchanan on November 5, 1936 in Butlerville, Indiana. The officiating minister was Rev. Joe M. Swarthoush. Juanita was born September 23, 1912 in Rush County.

Their children are as follows:

Rosalee Deloris Clarkson, born May 18, 1938 in Jennings County and died August 17, 2002 at age 64. She married Charles William Robbins on September 1957. Their children are Jeffery Charles Robbins, born July 26, 1960, Charlene Deloris Robbins, born October 25, 1962 (died 1963), Charla Kay Robbins, born May 12, 1965 and Cheryl Lee Robbins, born August 4, 1966.

Gene Allen Clarkson, born June 27, 1939 in Jennings County. He married Ruth Cann in 1957. They had two sons, Chris Allen Clarkson, born April 18, 1959 and Bennett William Clarkson, born June 18, 1962, died June of 2006.

Harold Albert Clarkson, born March 8, 1943 in Jennnings County. His children are Lisa Dana Clarkson, born September 25, 1962, Robin Denice Clarkson, born May 7, 1964 and Shane Harold Clarkson, born August 7, 1975.

Gerry Dean Clarkson, born January 20, 1945 in Jennings County. He married Phyllis Tuttle in May of 1964. Their children are Gerry Dewayne Clarkson, born March 21, 1965, Melissa Ann Clarkson, born October 18, 1968 and Troy M. Clarkson, born July 27, 1973.

Robert William Clarkson, born August 15, 1946 in Jennings County. His children are Tracie Lynn Clarkson, born June 25, 1969, Hollie Ann Clarkson, born June 28, 1971 and Romayne Alice Clarkson, born January 28, 1989.

Georgetta Clarkson was born February 11, 1950 in Jennings County and married Michael E. Gilmore on July 27, 1969. Her children are Brian Michael Gilmore, born January 28, 1974, Matthew Everett Gilmore, born June 22, 1977 and Jeremy William Gilmore, born September 23, 1983.

Dennis Ray Clarkson, born August 11, 1951 in Jackson County. His children are Jason Clarkson, born November 25, 1972 and Chad Clarkson born February 27, 1975.

*Peggy and Gerry both married persons related to Danny and I from other directions. Peg's husband, Bill, is our first cousin through our grandmother, Lavina Ziegler. Gerry's wife, Phyllis, is also descended through the line of Robert and Elizabeth Campbell.

Reflections on My Life and the Creek Called Wyaloosing

Together the woman and the bird saw the dawn creep in as she walked the deer paths along the meandering creek and the bird on silent wings skimmed the creek's surface, alert for a possible breakfast frog or fish.

The blue heron had been her ally for many a morning and they shared a special kinship. Perhaps the bird did not know it but the woman did.

It was here along the creek she had returned for healing. Here she had struggled to rebuild her life. Here she had wept in mind numbing grief for a son who would never come home and walk these paths with her.

But she had shared the trails with grandsons and taught them to skip rocks as they stood beneath the Sentinel, the Sycamore that had guarded the creek here at this spot for over sixty years. And as each year came and went, they would come again and again, selecting certain rocks with special shapes and tiny fossil imprints. But they never found an arrow head. But surely the arrowheads were there. She was sure Indians had camped here.

Yes, she believed long before her people had come, now almost two hundred years ago, there had been men who camped here, men of the Shawnee perhaps. It was as if at times through the years, she could feel their spirits, especially on days when she felt such a part of the land, men and women whom, she was sure, felt about this creek and this stretch of land as she did.

Now she wondered who would treasure this place as she had for over fifty years. Would it be one of her children's children or would this place go to someone else and would they feel as she had felt? Would they know the joy and peace she felt when visiting these woods and the creek? Would others find healing here?

It had been a special place for so long. She wanted others to experience what she had experienced. But she would have to leave it in God's hands. She must be confident that the creek and the land would speak to others as it had to her.

A Reflection on a Friend

Let the stillness of the morning
Seep into my soul
Touch my troubled heart
And heal my wounded soul.

I hear a songbird break the stillness
A woodpecker begins its drill
Answered by another
Like a dance of wills.

Here I sit this morning
In the woods we've both loved so long
Listening to the Wyaloosing
Roar along.

I've never seen her higher
Her banks are over flown,
But though her waters are troubled
My soul is troubled more.

For my friend is dying
And I grieve as I wait
For her to be summoned
Through heaven's pearly gates.

She's been my friend since I was seven
And that's nearly sixty years
She taught me from the Bible
In Sunday School and church.

Loralyn Reynolds

She walked with me down to the altar
Of our little country church
When I gave my heart to Jesus
And received a brand new birth.

And I wanted to walk with her
When she took this last long walk
And spend time with her
And have one more talk.

But she was in a hurry.
There was so much to do.
Her day was almost finished;
But I was confused!

So I must remember
The good times and all the love,
For she gave it in plenty
When I needed it in droves.

She always listened
With us she laughed and cried
And that is what I must remember
When I know that she has died.

For in living,
She loved me;
In dying,
There was only heaven on her mind!

Our Line of Reynolds, Renn, Thurston

Loralyn and Danny Reynolds

Father: Wilbur Reynolds

Grandfather: William Edwin Reynolds

Great Grandmother: Mary Ellen Renn

Great-great grandparents: Enoch Renn and Rebecca Thurston

Great-great-great grandparents: Henry Renn and Rachel Campbell;
Sylvanus Thurston and Lucinda Beers

G-g-g-g grandparents:Robert Campbell and Elizabeth
Moses Thurston and Catherine Bottemhomer
Eli and Susanna Beers

G-g-g-g-g: Israel Thurston

And so on to

John and Margaret Thurston

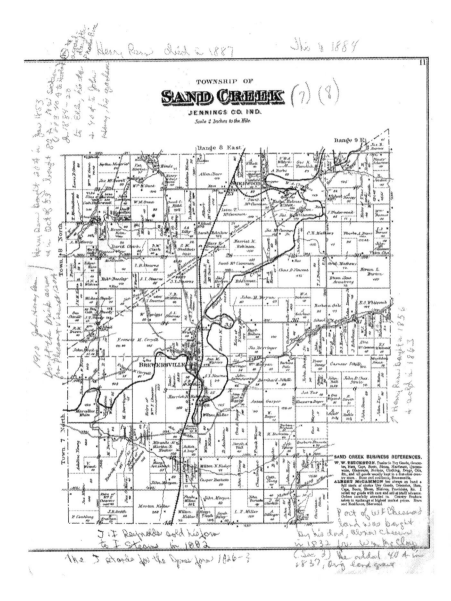

TOWNSHIP OF

SAND CREEK (7) (8)

JENNINGS CO. IND.

Scale 2 Inches to the Mile.

11

SAND CREEK BUSINESS REFERENCES.

W. W. THICKSTON, Dealer in Dry Goods, Groceries, Hats, Caps, Boots, Shoes, Hardware, Queensware, Glassware, Notions, Clothing, Drugs, Oils, &c., and all goods usually kept in a first-class country store. Store and residence, Brewersville.

ALBERT McCAMMON has always on hand a full stock of clocks Dry Goods, Groceries, Hats, Caps, Boots, Shoes, Notions, Provisions, &c. I select my goods with care and sell at small advance. Orders carefully attended to. Country Produce taken in exchange at highest market prices. Store and Residence, Sherwood.

The

REYNOLDS

FAMILY

ON

THE

BANKS

OF

SAND CREEK

Geneva

A Visit at Kellar Mill-1862

It was a busy morning for the mill, especially on a winter day. Bearded men stood around as they waited their turn for their grain to be ground. Of course, tobacco and talk flowed, especially talk about the war. For some were sure the war would be over before the next harvest. Others saw the handwriting on the wall. This was a war that should never have been fought, brother against brother. Brewesville had its share of southern sympathizers. And most families had relatives fighting on both sides. Every man had his opinion and freely shared it, but the old man most paid the greater attention to was David Reynolds, a man who had fought in a war, the war of 1812, and could add experience to opinion. David had come to the area in 1853, already an old man, but now even moreso. His farm was just up from the mill. The youngest man among them that morning was Eli Thurston, a seventeen year old barely shaving who would, in the next year, come to know the rigors of war. In the next decade, Eli's little seven year old niece, Mary Ellen Renn, after quite growing up, would marry David's grandson, Merritt Reynolds. But now none of that mattered. Another older man was respectively listed to. He was William Frank Cheever and was in the area before 1820, coming as a teenager with his dad from Vermont. The Cheevers had one of the earliest farms in the area and one of the biggest. It lay between the . and Fish Creek. Willie Frank's father, Abner, had fought also in the War of 1812 and Willie could remember what a difficult time his family had said it was. His mother, who he barely remembered, had hated that time. She had been bred for a gentler life, and war, and babies too close together, and too much work sent her to an early grave. He had been eight when his father remarried. His stepmother, Amy Wilson, was a kind woman, but she could never replace the lovely woman who was his mother. He said nothing of this as men around him discussed politics, the war, the price of grain, the weather. His oldest daughter, Almira, was married to David Reynolds' son, Joseph. Another daughter was married to Allen Parks and another to William Vawter. His greatest concern about the war was knowing, that if the months of fighting stretched into years, his son and son-in-laws would be probably be involved. He had three sons, but of course, only the healthiest would go to war. Of the other two, one had always been frail and the other was still and would always be a child. It was sad to think of losing all three and it could happen before his own death. He wasn't quite fifty, but he felt eighty. He went to check on his grain. He was eager to get home and to a warm fire and today was baking day. There should be fresh, and fragrant bread waiting. No one could beat his wife, Amelia, when it came to bread baking. And maybe, fresh butter had been churned. He wasn't a rich man, but he was better off than most of the men gathered there. Yes, he worked hard, but he also had had a better start with land his father had left him.

As he left with grain bags in tow, he nodded to another old timer, Henry Renn. Henry, like David Reynolds, had been in the area only since 1853, but he was older than Willie Frank. Both David and Henry had had farms in nearby Decatur County and didn't like the flat land. Henry's son, Enoch, was married to Eli Thurston's sister, Rebecca. Henry's farm was north of Brewersville, not on Sand Creek, but on a smaller stream, the Wyaloosing, that flowed down from Decatur County and then emptied into the Sand Creek to the west several miles. The two creeks often came rather close together. But the Sand Creek was navigable. The Wyaloosing was not. At least not for the kind of traffic that the mill sent out. Outside, Willie Frank searched the sky. The look of snow was there. He had hoped to have seen the last of it, but it had not been a bad winter. He had seen worse. The creek had frozen only for a short time, keeping the mill from operation. He flung the sacks into the two wheeled horse cart and climbed aboard. He spoke gently to the old and faithful horse, grey from birth and gray with age. The old horse slowly picked up his feet and started home. He knew the way. The man spit a long stream of tobacco and then settled down in a scrunch to try and pull as much warmth into his body as possible. Next time, he would send Abner, the son named for his grandfather and his father. He shortly remembered the lap robe and pulled it up from the cart and onto his lap. It was a weave of his own lady love and of his own wool, sheared by his own hand. Most farmers didn't like to mess with sheep, but he liked the critters, could eat their meat and enjoyed their wool. Above him a red tailed hawk circled. Then in a lighting fast dive and a squeak, the hawk had a snack. One less mouse in Sand Creek Township.

HN: No one in the mill that day could forsee that these forementioned men would some day share a family history page by becoming interconnected with the birth of the children of Merritt Reynolds and Mary Ellen Renn. The Cheever Farm was on Fish Creek. Marty Bryant owns part of it today. Part of the Reynolds farm is owned today by Clay and Nancy Burton. It is just barely south of Brewersville. Connected to the Cheever farm was the Jones' farm, the family of Amelia Jones Cheever, Willie's wife. (See following material on Cheever-Jones family.) The Kellar mill not only truly existed, but was one of the earliest mills in Jennings County. Adam Kellar came in 1814 before the county was a county or the state a state (both happening in 1816). He built a log cabin there and went and got his family. He obtained a government and state charter to build a mill and mill dam. Power for the mill was gained from an overshot water wheel. The mill was in full operation by 1823, grinding corn in the night and sawing lumber in the day. An Indian village existed nearby but they were friendly and stayed for several years, just one day silently left not to return. The mill was logs on a stone foundation. It was remodeled several times and finally destroyed in a flood in 1937. In 1921, it was claimed to be the oldest mill in operation in Indiana. It remained in the Kellar family the entire time, over a hundred years. It was of great importance to the growth of not only the local community but of the entire county. Some of the first state roads mention being laid out to pass Kellar's mill. In those early years, the mill flourished and so did the town of Brewersville, laid out by Jacob Brewer in 1837. Once it had two general stores, two doctors, an undertaker, a drugstore, a saloon, a blacksmith shop, a wagon shop; also a school and church. Also later there was built nearby a woolen mill. I am sure the inhabitants of the time expected it to continue to grow, especially when the Pennsylvania Railroad came through at the southern part of the town between the town and the mill. But by the time I remember it in the fifties, it was a sleepy little county town with only one country store, one two room school house and one small church and a couple handfuls of houses. It continued to decline until it loss the status of a town and now to strangers, it is just a wide place in the road where a few houses are gathered, but to us who remember, it is the place our friends went to school, where we visited at church, where we stopped to get a cold drink at the store on a hot summer afternoon after a swim in Sand Creek. It was the place I fell in love with two boys, (I've been in love a lot, never very seriously, obviously). One was red haired and stood head and shoulders above all the other fellas as he stood talking in front of the store. Our carload of wet kids, Becky (my best friend) driving, had just driven up. He never could remember my name so I just stayed a little bit in love with him for fifty years. The other was black haired and was one of the many boys showing off at the swim hole. He dated me on a bet with his cousin. They were always making bets. The joke was on him when he fell in love with me. We dated, were engaged, broke up, dated again, broke up, married other people, and finally realized we had had one of those once in a lifetime loves and by then it was too late. Did his death end my loving him? NO, it did not. I will always be grateful for his love. Like my great grandmother Reynolds before me and my great great grandmother Reynolds, I fell in love with a Brewersville boy. I just didn't have their wisdom to marry a local boy and stay put. I had to see the world. I chose interesting opposed to loving. I wanted both.

A Different Kind of Remembering!

ALONG THE SANDCREEK

"Tangled Roots"

Along Sand Creek, in the Kellar Cemetery at Brewersville, surrounded by giant trees and tangled roots, are eight relatively well marked graves of my father's family. Our family has been here for eight generations, the different lines coming between 1820 and 1853. The memorial stones represent the families Reynolds, Renn, Thurston, Cheever and Jones, Campbell, and Beers, and Penwell. That is a lot of tangled roots. Those are the names tangled by marriage and blood. Then add the Coryell name (that a great great aunt married) and the names of friends and neighbors. The Kellar name has been on documents related to my family for generations and Kellars have married distant cousins of mine. I went to school and 4H and church with the Kellars of my generation.

Most of the people buried in this small country cemetery represent hard working people with a serious work ethic and family values. However, my grandfather is buried here and was in an unmarked grave because he did not share those values. William Edwin Reynolds had seven children, one by his first wife, my grandmother, Lavina (Louvina) Ziegler, who divorced him in 1904 because of desertion, and six by his second wife, Elvia Muster. None of his children ever had anything good to say about him. Yet, he is my connecting link with these other family members, both the long dead and the many cousins such families produce. He was an alcoholic, and a womanizer, but he is still my grandfather. I never met him nor did I wish to. I had said for years that he did me a great favor and died before I was born. Perhaps he did. But I am not his judge. God is. And perhaps I have tried to live a decent life (and sometimes failed); not only because I have had a wonderful loving and supportive family, but because I did not want to be remembered by my children as my father remembered his father.

So after eighty years of lying in an unmarked grave, (he died in June of 1930) his grandchildren chose to place a simple marker on or near the grave of our grandfather, William Edwin Reynolds, not in love or fondness but in remembrance, that in his own way, he contributed to who we are today.

Some Early Reynolds Family History

I know very little about the early history of the Reynolds family. I have searched and researched working with my distant cousin, Jean Price, so that we could press farther back than David Uriah Reynolds, who we know is our great great great grandfather. We are pretty sure his father was Joseph Reynolds who settled in Franklin County, Indiana but pretty sure and well documented are not the same things. Both David and Joseph came from Orange County, New York, and about the same time to Franklin County. The age difference is suitable for father and son. Joseph had a brother named David. David named a son, Joseph, who turned out to be my great great grandfather. Our great aunt Edith indicated another ancestor named Joseph. David's son, John, is Jean's ancestor. John was several years older than Joseph, so there are probably other children, but of the Reynolds families living nearby at the time, I cannot find any firm documentation that links them. The names I mentioned include a Noah Reynolds and a Samuel Reynolds. My grandfather had a brother named Samuel but no other tie in except a land transaction. (In 1855 John Reynolds sold to Noah Reynolds lots in Brewersville and a store for $1,000.)

I found on Ancestry.com our David Reynolds. The source was a Melisssa Reynolds. She states that David's father was David Reynolds and mother was Elizabeth Smith. I cannot determine her accuracy. I, too found this David and Elizabeth Reynolds but could never find documentation that firmly linked our David Uriah to them, even though I was sure they were somehow related. They were in Orange County, New York at the same time. I will accept their marriage information re: David and Sarah. David and Sarah were married in Fayette County March 16, 1819. John was born in 1825 and Joseph in 1835, and no other children are mentioned, so perhaps they had only the two sons.

Also on Ancestory.com a Bendure Family site that gave James Reynolds (1748-1824) and Susannah Clark (1753) as parents of David.

The earliest Reynolds family in Jennings County according to my own research was the family of Patrick Reynolds. He is listed in the 1840 census, and is noted to have been born in Ireland. I would love to find some connection, but thus far, no luck. The origins of the Reynolds' family name is O' Reynold (Son of Reynold) and takes us to Leitrim Co. Ireland. However the name is considered Scoth Irish, and that could have happened in several ways.

The English kings were always trying to whip the Irish and the Scots into submission and through the centuries they tried several lawful but wrong ways to do so. One was giving away Irish land to the Scots. But even without government interference, there would have been the Scotch-Irish. The Irish married into Scottish families and the Scottish married into Irish families. I would like to think it could have happened to an early Reynolds' family as it did to our immediate family. I have found in one place where the O'Reynolds were a sub clan of the MacRandalls. That is a good description of our family. My grandmother married a Reynolds, who deserted her and she remarried a Randall, and brought into the Randall family a Reynolds son. But it was one Reynolds boy to three Randall boys, so sub clan.

However it happened, a Reynolds male left Scotland or Ireland or England sometime in the 1600s or 1700s and braved the large ocean in a little boat. I say little because those ships were not very big, and crowded and dirty and miserable at best.

Reynolds is a somewhat common name and early arrivals are found on ship logs, both sailing into Massachusetts and into Virginia. Our direct ancestor most likely sailed into Massachusetts because his family ended up in New York. By his obituary, we know David Reynolds was born in Orange County, New York in 1791. If Joseph is the father, he was born in Dutchess Co, New York in 1762 and fought in the war of Revolution, having moved to Orange Co. and enlisted from there, fought in New York line and boat series (this info comes from his pension file). He moved to Franklin CO., Indiana in 1811 or 1812. Father of this Joseph is Abraham. Joseph's wife is named Elizabeth and they are buried in Franklin County. IF this is the right line, it probably runs back to Robert Reynolds who was born in 1505 in Sanford, England. His son, Christopher, born 1530, with at least nine children, migrated to America with at least one son, William who was born 1560 in Kent, England. In 1637, William moved from Plymouth, Mass to R.I. His son, William, born 1603, had a son, James, born 1625, who died in R.I. in 1700. James son, Joseph, was born November 27, 1652. Joseph's son, Samuel, had a son named Thomas who had a son named Samuel, born 1752. This Samuel migrated to Eaton, New York. If that was spelled Etten, it would be in Chemung County, New York and that would be a connecting factor to our family. Some Revolutionary soldiers from Orange County moved to Chemung County (always westward), probably to use their military warrants.

David fought in War of 1812, came to Franklin CO., IN in 1815, to Decatur County by 1835 because his son, Joseph was born there. It is on 'The Letts Road' West. In 1853, they sold that farm and moved to Jennings County and bought a farm on Sand Creek, land lying on both sides of Brewersville. David's wife was Sarah Penwell. We thought they married in Franklin Co., but another researcher found the marriage record in Fayette County. They had two sons that we know of but there were probably others, especially since John and Joseph were so far apart in age (ten to twelve years). John also moved to Brewersville about the same time and bought the store which he sold shortly after. John was married to Rebecca Morgan in 1847. Their daughter, Samantha, kept journals including family history. John was a teacher (at one time had in his classroom the brothers, Orville and Wilbur Wright) and was also a minister. In 1855, he performed the wedding ceremony for his brother, Joseph, and pretty Almira Cheever, daughter of a well to do neighboring farmer, William Frank Cheever and Amelia Jones. (See Section on Cheever/Jones family). John Warren Reynolds and his wife, Rebecca also had a son named Robert J. and another daughter, Sarah and one named Molly. There may have been others. John looked a lot like his father. We have a picture of him but the picture we have of Joseph I., also states on the original picture that it is Morton Reynolds, which would have been

Joseph's son. It was a lady who gave the picture to the family that stated that the picture was Joseph Reynolds.???????

There on the Sand Creek farm, Joseph and Almira raised four sons and one daughter, Ida, who seems to never have married and is buried with her parents in the cemetery at North Vernon. The boys' names all started with an M. The oldest was Merritt Pinkey, my great grandfather. The others were Marion, Mahlon and Morton. There was another daughter who died as a child. Her name was Olive.

Sarah died in 1861. David died at the home of Joseph and Almira in August of 1874. He and Sarah are buried nearby in the Kellar cemetery with Olive. Scattered here and there in the small cemetery are other descendents. Merritt has two sons buried here, my grandfather, Edwin and his brother, Harry, who died as a child, four years old. There are also several in laws or out laws, depending on how one sees it. Marion's first wife is buried here, and perhaps Merritt's first wife who would have had the same name, Mary E Reynolds. But there is a marker for Marion's wife, but not for my great grandmother. Her father, Enoch Renn, is buried there and her sister and husband, The Coryells.

In 1882, Joseph sold most of the farm to Isaac Stearns. He had earlier sold twelve acres of the farm to Rebecca Thurston Renn, who was the mother of his daughter in law, Merritt's wife, Mary. That piece of land was part of the northern section of the farm and lay just out of Brewersville to the north just outside the town's limits near the school. After selling the farm, Joseph and Almira moved into town, that is either Vernon or North Vernon. According to census records, they were living in Vernon Township in 1900. They had a servant which may have meant that Almira was not well. The census record indicates that Joseph was a hackman driver, which was like a taxi with a horse. Both his sons, Marion and Morton, are living nearby, Marion working as a farmhand and Morton as a Leibryman (I think the census writer was inventive. I believe it was a livery stable.) My grandfather was working for him at the time and living with his uncle. Interestingly, Morton and his family are also caring at this time for Morton who is two years old and the son of Marion, whose wife had died. This, I believe was the third wife to die. Was the man just unlucky or did he tend to pick frail women?

His first wife was Mary E. Jordan, I believe Evert's mother. She died in 1887 when her son was five. IN 1889, he married Eliza Herron (who was a first cousin to Merrit's wife, Mary Ellen Renn). The obituary of Clarence, Marion's second son, says his mother was Margaret McCann. Clarence was born ten years after Evert, and a sister, Hazel, three years after that. Morton was born in 1898 and his mother died a few weeks later. Marion married Sarah Engle in July of 1898 but divorced her in October (per Plain Dealer). The marriage record indicates he married Alzora Ross April 20, 1904.

Marion's descendents remain in the area. His son, Morton, had six sons and one daughter. As much as I know about them, it is included in this section or I should say follows this section, listed as Marion Reynolds descendents. Marion died in 1942 and is buried at Vernon.

The other two brothers had children but I could not follow their families to this present generation. I did try. Mahlon died still rather young and as far as I can tell, had only one daughter. Her name was Zelpha and she married William Ashby 1908. I found them in Dearborn, Indiana in the 1930 census and found no more. She was born in January of 1884 or 1886 in Washington County, Indiana. Her mother's name was Amanda Goodman, also born in Washington County. Mahlon died in 1901 and is buried at the cemetery in Vernon. (1862-1901) and Amanda is also there (1861-1898).

Morton who married Clara Simmons, had three children listed in the 1900 census, Pearl, born July of 1887, Henry, born December of 1889 and Loella, born December of 1991. Pearl married Homer Harlow and remained in Jennings for quite awhile, ran a store/restaurant in Vernon at one time. Homer is actually in a picture with my great grandfather Ziegler. They were both working at some factory. I assume the spoke factory. In the 1940 census, Pearl and Homer are in Ft. Lauderdale, Florida. But they are buried at the cemetery in Vernon, Pearl, 1887-1949 and Homer, 1879-1968. Henry I also followed to Florida where I found his death record. Loella I found not a trace, and nothing more about the others.

The Family of Merritt Pinkey Reynolds

Merritt Pinkey Reynolds, my great grandfather and the first born son of Joseph and Almira Cheever Reynolds, was born in September of 1856, at the farm at Brewersville. His father bought the farm from his father in 1869 and had worked it with him since 1853.

Merritt married a local girl, Mary Ellen Renn, daughter of Enoch and Rebecca Thurston Renn in February of 1877. In 1879, Merritt bought land nearby from John Ditlinger but didn't keep it long. Merritt and Mary Ellen's five children were born near Brewesville. The five were William Edwin, my grandfather, born in August of 1878, Willard, born 1881, Harry born 1888 (who died at age four), Edith, born 1884 and Samuel Carl, 1890. By 1900, the census tells us that Merritt and his family were living in Center Township, still in Jennings County. He was working as a teamster at this time and they were renting a house. In this census, we are told all members of the household could read and write. In the next decade, a lot happens to this family. Evidently, Willard somehow found his way to Arkansas and goes to work for a logging company. Somewhere during this decade his father follows him and finds work there. He may also have found 'someone' there. It appears that way. Mary Ellen divorced him in 1911 and he remained in Arkansas and remarried. (1920 census, Jackson, AR, Merritt Reynolds, born IN 1855, spouse, Caroline Reynolds). He died in Arkansas in 1938, April 2, White County, and I assume he is buried there. His last job documented was at a Dairy farm.

Merritt's son, Willard, married a Mary Rutherford and had six children, Erma Jean, Helen, Cleo, Harry and Carl and Hilda. A man who went to church with Willard stated that Willard looked like Colonel Sanders. He also told me that of Willard's children, Harry married his aunt, Sadie Gober, his mother's sister, and Harry raised Sadie's daughters, Joanie Lee and Dorothy Freeman as his own daughters. Another child, Hilda, married a Solinger. Willard died and is buried in Arkansas. (1882-1971) (429-07-1625). Last known address: Monticello, Arkansas-according to the 1930 census. He was in a nursing home in Warren, Arkansas in the sixties when his sister, Edith, wrote to me. She was very gracious and gave me all the information she had at the time on family members.

She married Adrian McClain and had one daughter, Mary Louise Burnsworth. She and Uncle Sam lived most of their adult lives in Indianapolis and raised their families there. Uncle Sam, Samuel Carl Reynolds, married Nell Young, had one son, Herbert Carl (born April 23, 1914), who married Elma Merle Gatewood, had three sons, William Carl, James and Larry. William Carl was born September 10, 1942 and married Patsy D. Smith, (born May 12, 1943) on August 30, 1964. Their two children are Bradley William, born February 4, 1967 and Shari Teresa, born April 7, 1969. Bradley, married to Christie Donsbach, is the father of Alaina Rachel, born April 9, 1992 and Cole Benjamin, born March 5, 1998. I met William Carl and his wife in the nineties and they were living in Indianapolis.

James Robert Reynolds, was born January 29, 1947, married Janet Reasoner, had one son, Edward Scot, born August 5, 1967. Edward married Angela Sackett. James remarried, Sherra Witt, and had two more children, Barbara Christine, (Christy), born October 23, 1979 and Catherine Elizabeth, born August 11, 1987.

It is not clear but I believe my great-grandmother, Mary Ellen, died in Indianapolis at the home of one of her children. Her obituary says she died on Ferguson Street and is buried at Kellar cemetery but there is no record. Neither is there indication that she is buried with family members at Indianapolis. She died in 1929. Ferguson Street was the street that Aunt Edith lived on when she wrote to me, and on which Mary Ellen's grandson, Charles, lived on at a later time. Obviously, someone in the family was living there at the time of her death.

My grandfather, Edwin Reynolds, was working at Vernon and met my grandmother, Lavina (Louvina) Ziegler. I can see why he was attracted to her but not why she was attracted to him. He was already a heavy drinker, cocky and a braggart. Maybe she thought she could change him. She would not talk about it so I will never know. They were married Thanksgiving Day, November 28, 1901 at her parents' home in Vernon. Edwin was hardly ever home. But home enough to produce a child even though he rejected his first born son because of a crippled left hand. My father, Wilbur Alvadore Reynolds, was born December 17, 1902. They were living with Lavina's parents, Charles and Sarah Ziegler. Things went from bad to worse. One night Edwin threatened Charles with a knife. Charles told him to get out and not return. He just laughed and said he would come and go as he pleased. Obviously, he had not figured his father-in-law out, because he was never allowed to return to the Ziegler house. And all of Vernon sided with my grandmother. She divorced Edwin and gained custody of her son in 1904. She went to work at North Vernon and Sarah took over the care of baby Wilbur. She did keep in touch with Aunt Edith, who expressed interest in her nephew.

Also in 1904, Edwin gets his name in the paper again when twenty year old Alta Monroe commits suicide by taking carbolic acid. They had been courting and he had promised to marry her and then refused. At her death, she called for him and he came but was too late and drunk as well. Family tale passed down was that he was run out of town on a rail.

If he was run out of town, he must have returned. He remarried in 1910 to an Elvia Hastings, daughter of William Muster and Lulu Swartz. She was from Jennings County also. They had six children, Charles, (1910), Harry (1912, Mary (1913), Virgie Rebecca (1915), Tressie (1917) and Bob (1921). Interestingly, four of my grandfather's seven children were born in December. The family moved to Indianapolis after my grandfather's death in 1930. All six were born in Jennings County. Aunt Tressie was born in Jennings County in 1917 and she was next to the youngest. Edwin died in June and my father was notified. He did not intend to go to the funeral or see the other family. Great Aunt Edith convinced him to go. It was Aunt Tressie, still a little girl, who took my father's hand and walked with him up the hill to the cemetery at Brewersville. After the funeral, Uncle Sam talked to my dad and tried to talk him into moving to Indianapolis, said he would help him get work. He was sincere. He helped others in the family. But my dad was not interested. And thirty some years would pass before he would see any of his siblings again. One reason was my dad's attitude. The other reason was Elvia did not want her children to associate with their older brother. However, I tend to blunder in where angels fear to tread and I wrote to my aunts and uncles whose addresses Aunt Edith had provided. Only one responded. Aunt Tressie. And she came down several times to visit Dad. It was in the sixties and we knew he was dying. She was so open and warm. I believe her visits helped heal something in dad. We kept in touch for a long time. She was born in 1917, had married twice and had five children. Her married name was Condon. She was a teacher. Bob and Virgie never married, both lived with their brother, Charles and his family, until their deaths. Their mother also made her home with Charles. Virgie was very dedicated to her mother and spent her entire life working and helping Charles take care of their mother and family. Charles' wife, Lavina, was said to be an angel, patient and loving with such a large household. Bob had a childhood illness that prevented him from going past the third grade in school but he was very well read and very smart! He never had a full time job but helped with work around the house. Harry and Mary lived in southern Florida. Harry worked at the Post Office and had one son and one daughter. Mary married Don Shortemeier and had a son and a daughter.

In 2008, I made another stab at connecting with the Indianapolis part of the family. Much to my surprise, I got a call from Charles Reynolds, not my uncle, but his son, and my first cousin. A few months later, I got to meet with five of my first cousins: Barbara Lamb and Charles 'Chuck' Reynolds, the two children of Charles Reynolds, and Vonnie and her husband and her brother, Albert 'Doc' Condon, children of Aunt Tressie. We shared stories and pictures and it was a very special time for me. Vonnie lives in Florida but visits frequently. Doc lives near Indianapolis and so do Chuck and Barbara. Barbara, born September 19, 1946, has three children, Eric Edgar Lamb, born October 11, 1978, Kristin Renee Lamb, born November 13, 1981 and Jonathan Lamb, born October 18, 1983. Barbara has three grandchildren, Emily Kate Lamb (2012) and Oliver Marlowe (2011) and Charles Edgar Marlowe (2014). Chuck, born February 21, 1944, has three children, Samantha, born 1966 (adopted), Bryan VonAxelson, born 1969, and Shannon Reynolds, born February 14, 1980.

Re: Aunt Tressie's children. Vonnie has two children, and lives in Florida. She is married to Dan Lyons. Doc Condon (Albert) was born March 9, 1949. Aunt Tressie's youngest son, Bert, and oldest son, Keno

Davis, are deceased. Sylvia, another daughter, was married to a brother to Vonnie's husband. She had one son who died in his early twenties.

That is as far as I can go with the families of my first cousins.

So I will now put down my father's family-that is my brother Danny and his children and grandchildren and mine. My nieces promise to keep their section updated so I will leave space.

THE LANTERN

I have a little decorative lantern. It reminds me of my father.

I grew up in the country and on the farm. It was typical rural America of the mid 20th century. Electricity had only recently come to our area and only our house had been wired. The lantern was still the light that went to the barn and came back. Someway, somehow, that lantern became entwined with my father's love, with the security I grew to know was always there. He and the lantern always came back from the barn.

Throughout my life, in my darkest hours, I struggled with doubts and questions. Yet always, my heavenly Father came as the light that pushes back the darkness. Throughout all time, there have been darker periods but always a light persisted to pierce the darkness. The darkness or the dark one has never been able to totally destroy the light. John 1 translates the verse about light and darkness in different ways, and each is worth considering. Such as: "The light shineth in the darkness, and the darkness cannot comprehend it, cannot put it out, cannot overcome it, cannot extinguish it."

The Family of Wilbur A. Reynolds (first born son of first born son of Merritt Reynolds)

(including the amusing story of a soft-hearted woman and a tangled up mule)

William Edwin Reynolds' first born son was my father, Wilbur Alvadore Reynolds. They were both men of medium height, 5'8" or f' 9", medium built, 140 pounds average. This also pretty much describes Charles, (my dad's half brother) according to his son, 'Chuck'. My dad and uncle also had in common the early turning of their hair to white. My dad was the only son of Edwin Reynolds and Lavina (Louvina) Ziegler who divorced in 1904, both remarrying and giving my dad many half siblings.

My dad did not marry until he was forty-four years old. He married Nora Elizabeth Detamore in February of 1947. She was the daughter of a new neighbor with whom he had been working. He and Nora's father, 'Mick' Detamore, and Nora's brother, Phillip, 'Raggs' Detamore and her uncle, Jim Hoffman were all working on the road crew in Lovett township where they all lived at the time Nora and Wilbur met. Nora (born January 7, 1927) is the daughter of Percy O. Detamore and Madge Bell Highly). (See section on Reynolds-Detamore).

Nora and Wilbur went to Vernon to be married on Washington's Birthday but couldn't and returned to be married on February 24, 1947. They were married by Russell Calvert, mayor of Vernon. Mom wore a green dress with buttons down the front and dad wore a grey dress jacket. That evening the neighbors came to shivaree. Dad and Mom were living with Nora's dad on a farm west of Lovett. My dad loved to go on shivarees, so the crowd was most disappointed when my grandfather met them at the end of the lane with a shotgun, and a warning, which was very emphatic, "The first son o' bitch that steps on my property to shivaree my daughter and her husband will end up with an ass full of shot. My daughter is carrying a child and no harm will come to my grandchild if it is in my power to prevent it." Some muttering, some nodding in understanding, all subdued, they turned around and went back home.

But accidents will happen especially if you have a soft hearted woman and a tangled up mule. On a spring day a few weeks before my birth, my mother looked out to see that the mule was tangled up. My father and grandfather were at work and wouldn't be home for hours. So she went out to see if she could help. She ended up on her rounded tummy drug by the mule but except for being exceptional stubborn, I seemed not to suffer any ill from that experience. Of course, Mom got yelled at when she related the story. "What in the hell were you thinking of?" I guess you could say my grandfather was upset.

You already have an account of my unusual birth in April of 1947. If you haven't read it, it is at the beginning of the book, so don't fail to scan the event. My brother's birth was more normal and occurred seventeen months after on October 1, 1948. My mom had gone to her Aunt Pete's in expectation of the birth. I had been born on my due date so why not my brother? Yes, why not? Not only were we born on our due dates, but so was my oldest child, then it stopped. My boys were both late.

Anyway, my mother went into labor. My dad went for the doctor. Dr. Matthews arrived and found my mother in the middle of the living room embarrassed because she was standing in a puddle. Aunt Pete and she both realized that her water had broken and Aunt Pete had gone for some rags. Dr. Matthews put down his bag and picked my mother up, dumped her on the bed, set up in the living room for the purpose of this birth, and promptly fell over her. He was in his seventies at the time. SO maybe my brother's birth wasn't so boring after all? He was born a short time later, bundled up and laid on the couch, while my mother was attended to. Before he got moved, my grandfather came in and started to sit down on the couch and got yelled at by the doctor, my mother and Aunt Pete, "Don't sit on the baby". They never let him live it down. I remember him muttering at some family gathering when I was a teenager, and it was brought up by some family member, "I didn't come close to sitting on my grandson." Danny was born on a Friday evening.

Aunt Pete's farm was near my grandfather's in Lovett Township. We spent most holiday dinners there through the years, and other family gatherings.

Danny and my growing up years are found under the section on Growing up on the Banks of the Wyaloosing. I went to college in Kentucky in 1965, leaving home after graduating from Asbury and marriage to Charles Melvin in 1969. Thirteen months later, at the Baptist Hospital in Lexington, Kentucky, our first child, Christiana Marie Melvin, was born in the early morning hours, Saturday, September 12, 1970. She was a joy. She is now married to her third husband, Chad Caldwell, and lives in Sliver Hill, Alabama. Chad, born June of 1976, is the son of Buford Caldwell and Cheryl Stoner Payne, and the great grandson of James Stoner, who was a long time farmer in Sand Creek Township.

Christy is the mother of my two handsome grandsons, Dustin Darby Marshall, whose father is Dustin Shane Marshall. Darby was born Friday morning, November 30, 1990, in the hospital in Milton, Florida.

I was living in Milton at the time. My other grandson is Devin Dante Doyle, born Monday, October 9, 1995 in Columbus, Indiana. We were all living in North Vernon at the time. Devin's dad, Bobby Doyle was Christy's second husband.

My children's father, Charles Melvin, was born in North Carolina in August of 1944, but he is from Northwest Florida. He and his mother and grandmother left North Carolina on a train when he was just a few days old to return to their Florida home while his army dad left for Europe to join the push to defeat Hitler. His parents were Mary Dalton and Whitfield Melvin.

Our second child, Charles Clay (Clay) was born in South Boston, Virginia on December 23, 1973, a son. He was Sunday's child. I was in shock at his birth even though I now realize his birth defect was very minor. It did make feeding difficult. And he had to have three surgeries in that first two years. Clay was born with a bilateral cleft of the lips and hard and soft palate. He was an adorable but hyperactive little boy that turned his all boy type of personality to sports and scouts. He was an eagle scout and MVP in high school sports. He played both soccer and ran cross country and track. After an year of college, he joined the Air Force in 1993 and married his high school sweetheart, Sonia Androskaut in that same year. He did well in the Air Force but was looking forward to coming home. He had a special affinity and connection with all of us. He and Sonia were separated when he was killed in an accident in Japan near where he was stationed at Misawa. The date was July 6, 1996. He was brought back to be buried at the Naval Air Station in Pensacola, an area he loved, but of course, he isn't really there. En route, he was accompanied by his closest friend, then a marine, Robert Pitts. Rob helped us and still helps us remember and be grateful for what we had.

Our youngest son, Daniel Warren, was born Thursday, July 14, 1983 in Naples, Italy. He was delivered by the woman that would become one of my dearest friends, navy doctor, Dr. Penelope Maynard. Our Daniel was born at the Naval Hospital and at nine pounds and twelve ounces, he was referred to as the elephant of the nursery. He became the focus of all our lives. Daniel is married to Krysta Thompson (born August of

1983) who has a son, Aydan, who is eleven years old, born in October of 2002. Aydan's father is Matt Arrington.

I have been divorced since 1990 and after obtaining a second degree, (this time, from the University of West Florida) came back to Indiana to live in 1993. I worked in Social Services for the State of Indiana from 1996 to 2007, took disability in 2007 because of my struggle with Parkinson.

My brother, Danny, finished his Army stint in 1971. He was in Germany several months. After he got home, he began to seriously date Jean Taylor Dixon, a young widow who lived in the trailer court where Mom lived. She and Mom had become friends. Jean is the daughter of Georgia and Dewey Lee Taylor and was born January 23, 1949. She and Danny were married in 1977 and their daughter, Chatney, was born February 16, 1978. The next year added Season Amber on the 31st of May. (Both born in Columbus, Indiana) Danny and Jean almost lost Season when she was seven, a Wilma tumor was discovered. During treatment, she struggled when the cancer spread to her lungs. Because of her intensive chemotherapy, doctors warned her she may not be able to have children but her daughter, Georgia Elizabeth was born May 1, 2008 and son, Langer Clay, in June of 2012. She is married to Gregory Bassett, the son of Gregory and Cheryl Bassett. Gregg was born November 28, 1981. He has a son, Loy, born in 2006.

Chatney was born a social butterfly and her daddy's ball player. She was actively involved in school, sports, and with her family and friends. After graduation from North High School in Columbus, Indiana, she picked up a cosmetology license while working on her college degree and began her Mary Kay business during this time as well. She married Justin Gelfius in November of 2001 and has Crew Warren, born December 18, 2004, Ledger William, September 20, 2006, Charleston Grace, born May 7, 2008 and Grane born August 17, 2012. Justin farms on a large scale and Chatney is a high level consultant with Mary Kay. Justin is the son of William and Norma Gelfius and was born in June of 1978.

Jean and Danny are now both retired. HA!! Danny retired from Columbus based Cummins in 2003 and started a lawn business that is triple what he had in mind as a part time job after retirement. He also bought rental units and fixed them up for fun, tries to rent to people he knows or people who know people he knows. He still plays ball, can still hit a ball way out there but is having trouble with the running part. He has managed a ball team for the last several years. The important thing is that he still enjoys it. Jean retired from Columbus' school system or rather Bartholomew County Public Schools. She taught for twenty years for the public school system and for several years for a private school. While the girls were little, she worked at home. She now works on developing her Mary Kay business and on enjoying her grandchildren, and helping out with extended family (that's us).

(Leave Space for family additions)

Reynolds Documentation and Tidbits

Newspaper Gleanings

Obituary/David Reynolds from Plain Dealer, September 8, 1874

At the residence of his son, J. I. Reynolds, at Brewersville on Saturday, August 29, 1874, Mr. David Reynolds, of paralysis, age 83 years, 5 months and 27 days. Mr. Reynolds was born in Orange County, New York, was a soldier in the War of 1812, and came to this state in 1815 and to this county in 1853 settling at Brewersville where he has resided ever since. He was a worthy citizen and well respected.

Obituary/Joseph I Reynolds from North Vernon Sun, May 13, 1920

Joseph I. Reynolds died of pneumonia after an illness of only four days. He was the son of David Reynolds, born in Decatur County February 17th, 1835, being eighty-five years, two months and twenty-two days. He was united in marriage to Almira A. Cheever August 19, 1855, from which union six children were born, four sons and two daughters. Three sons, Morton H, Merritt P., and Marion O. Reynolds are left to mourn his departure. He leaves a large number of grandchildren and twenty-six great grandchildren. He united with the church at the age of twenty and was a faithful attendant until the last few years on account of his advanced age it was difficult for him to hear. He moved from Decatur County to Jennings at an early age and he was one of the pioneers of the county. He was here when this part of the country was mostly woods and helped blaze the trails for our present roads. He was farmer, contractor and merchant, but always preferred the outdoor farm life and to this he attributed his strong constitution and good health. He was never sick until his fatal illness and never had a fever until that time. Many times he has made the statement that his life covered an epoch in world history and scientific advancement that only very few were privileged to witness. He had seen the boundary of our present country grow and the rise and fall of empires. He loved to contrast the days of the ox drawn plow to the modern tractor, the Indian signal fires on the hills to our modern wireless system, the day of walking to our aerial express, and the hardships of the old log cabin to the comforts of our modern homes. He was always a student. Mr. Reynolds joined the Masonic Lodge at Westport December 18, 1858. He later was admitted to North Vernon Lodge NO. 59 and was an active member at the time of his death. He was a member of this order for over sixty years. He was a firm believer in the teachings of this order and his faithful attendance made him well known in Masonic bodies.

Plain Dealer: J.I. Reynolds died 1920 at home of granddaughter, Mrs. Homer Harlow. Survivors: Morton H., Merritt of Arkansas and Marion O. of Anderson.

At the Old Johnson's Fork Baptist Church Cemetery in Franklin County: Joseph Reynolds, born February 11, 1762, Died May 4, 1846. 84 years, two months. Wife Elizabeth, born August 24, 1769; Died 1843.

From the book, Revolutionary War Pension Files, we find Joseph Reynolds, New York line and New York Boat Service, S 31928, sol born 11 Jan 1762 in Dutchess Co., New York and lived in Orange CO, New York at enlistment, in 1802 moved to Ontario Co, New York and in 1811 to Franklin Co., IN where he applied 12 May 1834, a resident of Whitewater twp.

Form the Plain Dealer, April 6, 1911, Circuit Court Notes: A divorce was granted to Mrs. Mary Reynolds from her husband, M. P. Reynolds.

Banner Plain Dealer, April 4, 1902 J.R. Collins has brought the dray of Everett Reynolds.

Banner Plain Dealer, February 20, 1901 Vernon: Morton Reynolds nominated for councilman, Democratic ticket. William McKinley was reelected president of the United States last Wednesday and Theodore Roosevelt declared vice-president by the Electoral college. For sale: Pure stock Plymouth Rock eggs, $1 per dozen-John Childs

Banner Plain Dealer, December 20, 1901, Vernon, Mahlon Reynolds, 40, died of cancer on Wednesday, December 11

Banner Plain Dealer, January 19, 1898, Vernon: The wife of Mahlon Reynolds died at her home early Wednesday morning

Banner Plain Dealer, February 23, 1898 Grayford, Born on February 16, 1898 to Marion Reynolds and wife, a son

Banner Plain Dealer, April 13, 1898 The wife of Marion Reynolds, a former resident of North Vernon but recently of the southern part of the county, died of consumption at her home near Freedom Church last Saturday morning.

Banner Plain Dealer, October 6, 1904 North Vernon, Owing to needed and extensive repairs being made at the electric light plant, the lights have been shut off for the past few nights, making the town seem dark as a dungeon.

Plain Dealer, June 6, 1907, Sunday morning the second section of freight train NO. 63 on the Big Four Railroad was wrecked near Brewersville delaying traffic many hours

Plain Dealer, March 12, 1914, Lonesome Corner, Everett Reynolds remains quite poorly.

The Family of Marion Reynolds

Marion Reynolds was the second son of Joseph and Almira Cheever Reynolds, born September of 1860, on the farm near Brewersville, Indiana. He married Mary E. Jordan, August 4, 1881. She died in 1887 (is buried at Brewersville). I assume she is Evertt's mother. He married Elisa Herron in 1889. She was a cousin to his sister-in-law, Mary Ellen Renn Reynolds. I assume Eliza died. His son, Clarence's obituary, and Morton's state that their mother was Margaret McCann. She died weeks after Morton's birth (1898). There was also a daughter, Hazel, born three years after Clarence. According to the Banner/Plain Dealer, he remarried in July of 1898 to a Sarah Engle and divorced her in October of same year. In 1904, he married Alzora Ross. In the 1900 census we find Morton living with his Uncle Mort, makes sense if Marion didn't have a wife at the time. In this census Marion is listed as a farmhand, and listed with three children, Evertt at seventeen, Clarence at seven, and Hazel at four. He was living in Anderson when his father died per obituary (1920). Marion died in 1942 and is buried at Vernon. His son, Clarence, was born January 17, 1893, served in WWI, was a brick layer, a member of the Baptist Church and of the Masonic Lodge. He died at 90 in 1983 in North Vernon.

It is Marion's son Morton Reynolds that I know the most about. His descendents are numerous in Jennings County and round about counties. His offspring include Lee Reynolds, Kenneth Reynolds, Ray Reynolds, Paul Richard Reynolds, William Reynolds, and Alice Reynolds. Also a Clarence Reynolds. Morton was married to Ora Kelly. He died in 1973 and is buried at Vernon.

Kenneth, Ray (1933-1992), Paul Richard, and William are all deceased. The following is what I know about their families. I have met several of their children and grand children.

(1) Lee, Married to Mildred, have daughters {1} Mildred (Marie) married to Buck Perry, two children, Allen Perry, two sons, B.J. Perry and Jordan Perry and Julie who is married to Bill Hardebeck

and has two children, Jessie Ballenger and Daniel Ballenger. {2} Linda born in 1946, married to Jerry Lamb, three daughters, Tonja Lea married to Philip Marsh, has four children, Alexandra Leigh (1995) and Tucker Allen (1998) and Sadie Elizabeth and Levi. Philip is the son of Paul Marsh and the grandson of Norval and Alberta Marsh. Jerry and Linda's daughter, Lisa is married to Doug Hudson and they have three children, Darby Hudson (2005) and Carter Hudson (2008) and Ivy Jean Hudson (2013). Krista, Linda's third daughter, is married to Bryan Lane. {3} Marcia is married to Jamie Olds and has two sons, Jamie and Jacob Olds. Lee has a great-great grandson, Seth.

(2) Kenneth, Married Martha, had four children as follows {1}Chris Reynolds married Maddox, has three children, Christine (with daughter, Carla), Anita and Linda (whom I have met). {2}Carolyn Reynolds married Garris, has two children, Larry Garris and Amy Petro with daughter, Rebecca. {3} Alfred Reynolds has four children, Joyce, (whom I have met), Alfred, Jr. (Sketter), D. J. and Susan. {4} Kenneth Albert who has no children.

(3) Ray was first married to Patty Porter and had two children, one was Timothy, now deceased. Ray remarried and had stepchildren that he helped raise.

(4) William, had two daughters

(5) Paul Richard, Married to Marilyn, had two children. {1}Paul {2} Lisa, (born 1968) married to Lonnie Clymer. Paul, JR lost his wife, Melissa in 2009. Granddaughter, MaKayla Stallard.

(6) Clarence

(7) Alice, who married Robert Amis, has two children, {1}Tammy and {2} Robert. Tammy has a son, Jonathan Giddens.

Our Reynolds Line

Danny and Loralyn Reynolds
Father: Wilbur Reynolds
Grandfather: William Edwin Reynolds
Great grandparents: Merritt Reynolds and Mary Ellen Renn
Great-great grandparents: Joseph I. Reynolds and Almira Cheever
Great-great-great grandparents: David Reynolds and Sarah Penwell
William Frank Cheever and Amelia Jones
4-great grandparents: Abner Cheever and?
George and Prudance Jones

THE CHEEVER-JONES FAMILY

ON

THE

BANKS

OF

FISH CREEK

Fire of Heaven

Come, O Come, Fire of Heaven
Come, O Come, Living Flame
Come and burn away the dross
Let the silver only remain.

Then, Lord, from the silver
Fashion a vessel
According to your need
And fill with the Holy Spirit
And make your will plain.

Come, O Come, Fire of Heaven
Come, O Come, Living Flame

Come and hold sway over us
So nought but you remain
So your will be done on earth
As in heaven
Oh, come, Living Flame.

Come, O Come, Fire of Heaven
Come, O Come, Living Flame
Come and burn away the dross
Let the silver only remain.

Amelia Jones Cheever

The light of a new day steadily stole away the darkness and pushed away the heavy mist that had hugged the land.

Corn still stood in the surrounding fields but it was harvest time and in a few days there would be only acres of golden stubble.

So it was. So it had been. 'Springtime and autumn, seedtime and harvest, great is thy faithfulness, Lord, even unto me.' She thought about the time she had discovered the words of Jeremiah, words and thoughts that had come to him when imprisoned in a dank, dark well. He had been complaining about his lot when the tone of his prayer changed, and the prophet said, "When I remember, when I recall to my mind, when I make to return to my heart, then I have hope. His mercies are new every morning. The Lord is my portion, says my soul. I will hope in him. I will wait for Him. Great is thy faithfulness, Lord, even unto me."

There was something increasingly reassuring now, as she grew older, about the sameness of things, the rotation of the seasons, births and deaths in their cycle, 'a time to be born and a time to die.'

She had come up from Virginia to the young state of Indiana with her parents in 1818. She had been born in Virginia in 1815. She remembered only fleetingly of the trip. They had come with her Uncle William and his family. They hadn't come to Jennings County first but lived a short time in both Jackson and Bartholomew Counties. But when she was eleven, her folks found a place they liked on Fish Creek and they moved to the farm there and there within the radius of a mile, she spent the rest of her life.

The Cheever family were their nearest neighbors and Willie Frank was just a year older. They were friends from the beginning. She married William Frank Cheever in June of 1834. She was 19 years old. Her brother, William married Sarah Conners three days before. The Circuit rider, Joshua Law, performed the ceremonies. When a minister was handy, it was not unusual for there to be several weddings and baptisms.

HN: W. F. was the oldest Cheever son and worked closely with his father, Abner, who was one of the earliest landowners in what would be Sand Creek township. W.F. had two younger brothers and two sisters. His mother had died, and the youngest two were Amy's whom his father had married in 1822 in Jennings County. W.F. had been born in Vermont and his father was from Massachusetts, and had fought in the War of 1812. Abner Hersey Cheever was born in 1787, Jan 14 to Dr. Samuel Cheever in Boston, MA. Interesting, in my research, I have found that the name, Abner Cheever, was very common in the east, but this is the only date that fits our Abner.)

W.F. inherited most of Abner's holdings, which included land bought in a cash sale in 1820. He and Amelia added to the farm including some of the Jones' land. They worked hard and cared for their aging parents. Amelia's parents were George and Prudance Jones, born respectively 1778 and 1784 in Virginia. They were people of tenacious faith and she had taken that for herself. She was active in the Fish Creek Society, a group of Christians that met in homes until a church could be established. Finally, a church was established in Brewersville-a United Brethren congregation served by a circuit rider who made his rounds on horseback and stayed with local families a few days each time he came.

W. F. and Amelia were parents of eight children. Their daughter, Mary Jane married Allen Parks; their daughter, Angie, William Vawter, one of the descendents of the Vawters that settled and platted the small town of Vernon, the county seat of Jennings County. Their Almira married Joseph I. Reynolds and thusly became my great-great grandmother. The only Cheever son to marry was William Abner who married Clara Stearns. He bought a farm north of his parents. It was nearly on the Decatur-Jennings line on the Sand Creek. He and his wife are buried in the McCammon cemetery in that area. He had many descendents including Ken Cheever who farmed in Sand Creek and attended the New Bethel Church. Also one of his descendents, Cora Cheever married Clay Beesley, whose daughter, Gail married Walter Carpenter. Gail's children attended church with us at Pleasant View. (A separate paper is attached with more information on this line.)

It appears from scanty records that the other 4 children did not marry. There was a James and an Amelia and a Horace born about 1852. Daughter Amelia died in 1876 at age 26 and Horace in 1872 at 20. They are buried in the Fish Creek Cemetery as are W. F. and Amelia and Amelia's dad, George Jones. Her mother is probably there as well but I found no record of it. The cemetery is small but lies near State Road 3 and is easy to find. You take a narrow road to the right past the Sand Creek School. You go only a few yards, park your car and take a hike. It is parallel with the highway, a little bit hidden by trees.) W. F. died in 1874. He was only 60 years old. Amelia lived until 1899. She was 84 years old. Note that she had outlived a husband by 25 years and four of her eight children. Three losses came relatively close together, 1872, 1874 and 1876.

She is one of the ancestors I feel a bond with. She may not have been the person I think her to be, but my summation of her life is based on the study of census records, her obituary, newspaper clippings, the history of Sand Creek Township, a publication by the EUB church, marriage and land records, visits to her grave and to the farms of both the Jones and Cheevers. I believe she was a woman of great faith, who believed in hard work and family, the kind of woman I aspire to be.

Cheever/Jones Research Notes

Summary re Cheever Research

Interview with Kenneth Cheever-

Kenny farmed in Sand Creek township and attended the New Bethel Church. He and his wife, Martha, had one son, Jim who lives in the St. Louis, Missouri area. Kenny's brothers and sisters include William F. who lived in Galveston, IN and died in 2000. There was also Mary Louise who married a William McCawley and lived in Kokomo and a Frances Evelyn. Ken's father was Frank W Cheever and he is buried in Kokomo. Frank's siblings include Audrey, Eldo, Inez, Cora and Clestie. Ken's Grandfather was John W. Cheever and his siblings incude Clifford, Evertt, Ollie, Stella and Cora. Ollie married a Charles Johnson and one of their children, Howard, lived near Ken. Howard's son lived in FL. There was also a Wilbur Johnson who lived in Indianapolis and a Cheryl who married a Grable and lived at Noblesville.

One of the Cora Cheevers married Clay Beesley, Herb Beesley's uncle. They had two daughters. Their daughter, Gail married Walter Carpenter and they lived on the Clay Beesley farm. Their children, a son, Dale and a daughter, Evelyn, and a son, Robert, attended the Pleasant View Church during the time we did. Evelyn was married to a Katzenmeyer and has a son named James. She is now married to Leon Fair and lives in Seymour. Bob lives there, too. Hazel lived in New Castle. (I found an obituary that indicates that Walter and Gail lost a child in 1936. It so reads: Donald Carpenter, age 1, died of whooping cough. Friday, June 26. Funeral at Pleasant View. Son of Walter and Gayle Carpenter. Minister: Wayne Smith. Other survivors include Brother Dale and grandfather Henry Clay Beesley and Grandmother Linda Carpenter.)

Clifford Cheever had a son named Harry who lived in North Vernon. A Clifford Cheever 1877-1955 is buried in Mt Arie Cemetery in Decatur Co.

Ken's great grandfather was William Abner Cheever who was a brother to our great-great grandmother, Almira Cheever Reynolds. This would have made Dad and Kenny 5th cousins and Jim our generation. Wm A is buried in the McCammon Cemetery, a cemetery almost on the Decatur Co line.

This concludes the interview with Ken Cheever. I wish I could remember the date but I believe it was back in the 70s.

Addition: 2008 obit: NV PD: Death of William Cheever, 78, at Galveston, funeral attended by nephew Jim Cheever, (son of Kenneth Cheever) of St Louis, MO area. Other survivors include a son and daughter with grandchildren.

2009 Research-JC Library

Obituary of Amelia Cheever

Amelia (Jones) Cheever died May 8, 1899. Born in VA Jan 23, 1815, came to Sandcreek township with her parents. Age 84. Married William F. Cheever 1834. 8 children, 3 sons and one daughter dead. One son and 3 daughters living. (Submitted by Wm A Cheever, June 2 1899)

Obit of Amelia Cheever Died: Miss Amelia Cheever, March 5, 1876. Age 26. Burial: Fish Creek (youngest daughter of W F and Amelia Jones Cheever.)

Newspaper clippings:

April 30, 1872 Horace Cheeveer died (son of WF and Amelia)

March 12, 1872 Amy Cheever, dec AD: Daniel Bacon {this was the 2nd wife of the Abner Cheever who was the father of WF. She married in 1822 in Jennings Co and was Amy Wilson.—JC marriage record}

Andre Cheever—age 17, died 1904, son of John and Lizzie Cheever, buried at Brewersville.

1864 Income tax record:

    WF Cheever $11.65
    George Jones $7.85
    John Kellar $14.00

Marriage record   Amelia Jones to W. F. Cheever, June 15, 1834
                  William A Jones to Sarah Ann Conner, June 12, 1834
                  (married by J. Law)

1860 Census Sandcreek Township Jennings CO Indiana

William Cheever	45 Value $3,000.00
Amelia	45
Mary	21
Wm Abner	19
Angeline	17
James M	15
Amelia A	10
Horace I	8
Wm Riggs	21 Milling

1850 census

William F Cheever	35	farmer 800	Vermont
Amelia	35		Virginia
Almira	14		Indiana
Mary J	11		"
William A	10		"
Angeline	7		"
James M	5		"
Amelia A	6 mos		

1840 Census JC

Franklin Cheever

Loralyn Reynolds

{ a Samuel Cheever listed in 1840 census, Kosc Co)

1830 Census Jennings Co

Abner (F or H) Cheever (one male listed 40-50 yrs old, one female 30 to 40 years old, a male and a female between the ages of 15 and 20 and a male and female between the ages of 10 and 15 and a male under 5)

In 1820 census an Abner Cheever is listed with 3 children, all under 10. All this fits with W. F. who was born in 1814. There was no wife then. She either died enroute or shortly after arriving in IN. A Joshua Cheever is also listed in the 1820 Jennings census, is in the same age range with a wife and two small children.

Land Records—Library and Courthouse (Research from 1998 to 2009)

Abner Cheever had Section 3 (Sandcreek township-even though it wasn't a township yet) land purchased with cash, cash entry sale, April 24, 1820, Jeffersonville land office.

Abner Cheever, August 1, 1839, 40 acres, Jeffersonville land office.

Wm McCloy to Abner H Cheever May 29, 1832 for $100.00, part of SW qrt. of section 3, 7, 8. It was recorded June 18, 1934.

Gorge Jones bought 160 acres Feb 4, 1826 from Isaac Holeman. It was the NE quarter of section 9, 7, 8. The land adjoined Cheever land.

1825 Cash sale for land in Bartholomew Co for George Jones

1850 census lists a George B. and Prudance Jones and Nancy Heary who is 48. Prudance is 66 and George born about 1778 in VA. It puts them in Geneva township.

In 1835, George bought another 40 acres of land in Jennings.

In 1837, William F Cheever bought 40 acres, SW qtr of SW qtr, section 3, 7, 8

George Jones 40 A LO Jeffersonville; Issue date 11-9-1841

George D Jones from Wm Jones Feb 12, 1844 for $50.00 N ½ SW qtr of NW qtr 10, 7,8 20 acres. Book L p 512 R: June 11, 1850

George D Jones from George Jones Aug 14, 1845 for $50.00 NW qtr 10, 7,8; 40 A; Book L, p 513; R: June 12, 1850

George D. Jones fr Willis Thickston April 28, 1857; NW NE 36,8,8 40A; Book U, p 322; R: May 27, 1857

George Jones from Willis Thickston Aug 11, 1857; NW E ½ NW 36, 8,8 20 A R; Sept 9, 1857; Book U

(I can only guess that this George D. Jones was a son of George and brother to Amelia. I would like to follow this line but have no clue if they moved, stayed and changed names or evolved in some other way.)

A man named Day bought land off WF Cheever in?. E ½ NW 9,7,8 80 acres.

MORE CHEEVER/JONES TRIVIA
FROM 2009/2010 RESEARCH

Marriage records: Ollie Cheever, daughter of W. A. Cheever and CF Stearns marries Charles B. Johnson, son of A P Johnson on January 24, 1884.

William A. Jones to Sarah Ann Conners, June 12, 1834 by Joshua Law or Low
William F. Cheever to Amelia Jones, June 15, 1834 by Joshua Low or Law
George D. Jones to Sarah J. Brougher, August 1841 by John Johnson, MG

James Jones to Susasnna Kellar, May 12, 1838 by W Gaddy, JP
James Jones to Amanda Campbell, April 27, 1837

Margaret Jones to Tim Linder, 1837
Drucilla or Priscilla Jones to Jackson Clarkson, Sep 1841
Lorinza Jones to WM Walker, Dec of 1840
Mary Jones to Obadiah Hand, May of 1839
E Jones to J Walker, 1841
Jonathan Jones to Delia Kellar, Oct 16, 1841, by John L. Johnson< MG (These above are listed because of the like hood that they were cousins or siblings of Amelia Jones. Especially George D. Jones and James Jones, and Jonathan Jones, who owned land near the other Jones farms and any marriage to a Kellar places one near Brewersville. There appears to have been at least two James Jones of the near age). Land records indicate that in this time period, Section nine had the following owners: Wm Jones, George Jones, a Coryell, a Wildley. Section 10 was shared by George Jones, James K Jones, James N. Jones, Wm A Jones, Jonathan Jones, Daniel Jones, a Smith, Jacob Kellar, and Elias Brewer.

In 1824, Abner Cheever, Esquire, officiated at the wedding of Samuel Wilson and Sarah Chapman. (Abner's second wife was Amy Wilson; I assume this Samuel was a brother.)

William A Cheever to Clara F Stearns, Oct 22, 1865, by JL Stearns, VOM

WILLS

THERE are wills related to this family, and as follows: Amelia A. Cheever, Will Book 3, pp. 18 & 19 (1876). It lists brothers and sisters as Wm A. Cheever, James Cheever, Almira A. Reynolds, Mary Jane Parks, and Angeline Vawter, witnessed by Wilton and Nancy Kellar. There ia also James Cheever, Will book 3, pp 46-48, 1876, and Wm F Cheever, Will book 2, pp 379-81. (1874)

W A CHEEVER-MILITARY INFO-Prv Co I 33 Reg IN Volunteers, War of 1861-1865; five children under 16; living in Harper, IN, requesting pension for rupture sustained while serving in Atlanta, GA in 1864 and Rheumatism as a result of chronic diarrhea.

NEWSPAPER GLEANINGS
RELATED TO JONES/CHEEVER

Abner Cheever, robbed on Bear Creek,	Apr. 6, 1887 (PD)
W. A. Cheever buys property " ",	June 4, 1884 (PD)
Jones Farm sells, Brewersville	Apr 21, 1886 PD
" House	Jan 14, 1885 PD
Ms Nellie Jones visit Fish Creek	Jan 10, 1884 PD
Merritt Reynolds visiting	Jan 10, 1884 PD

FROM VAWTER HISTORY—(Buchell) Angeline E Cheever, born 7-24-1842 at Brewersville, married William A Vawter, son of Jesse and Sarah Parks Vawter. Wm was born July 13, 1842. They married in 1861. He enlisted and served in Co 82 Reg IN volunteers until close of war, never wounded or sick-took place in battles of Perryville, Ky, Stone River, TN, Chickamauga, Lookout Mountain, Missionary Ridge— Peach Tree Creek (GA), Atlanta, returned to farm and later went to Edna, KS Children: Amelia F. Vawter born 1862 married HL Hatton, lived in KS and Clara Vawter born 1865 married Bowen Heath, also lived in KS (Labette Co)

Wm Vawter's father was Jesse, son of Wm and Frances Vawter Vawter (yes, she was a cousin). Jesse's father, William, was a brother to John Vawter, who found the town of Vernon. (So our great, great great aunt Angie was married to a man whose grandfather was a brother to Vernon's founding father.) Jesse R. Vawter had a cabin on Fish Creek 1840 and lived there two years before moving. (So I can only assume that William was born on Fish creek.) He had 8 siblings. Jesse was also named after his grandfather.

SIDE NOTE—Wm Vawter served in the same Civil War company as our great great great uncle, Eli Thurston who is the great-grandfather of Georgetta Clarkson Gilmore.

From Vernon to Madison-3 day trip with packhorses; 8 dimes to a dollar; corn 12 and 1/2

Cents a bushel; chickens at 50 cents a dozen; milk cow $7; wheat 37 and ½ cents a bushel; 6 bits for coffee; 6 bits for cotton goods; 3 bits a day for labor; split rails 25 cents for a hundred (1835)

Banner plain Dealer, November 10, 1897, While at Vernon . . . we heard a tale to the effect that Commissioner Cheever had asserted he would build the contemplated bridge to connect his farm with Decatur County or 'bust' and that Treasurer Trapp had intimated he would 'bust'. The Tripton Mills were paying 88 cents a bushel for wheat yesterday.

*The next sections are a few stories and details from my father's mother's family, stories of the Zieglers, the Arneys, the Davis families and my great great grandmother Sarah Catherine Schneider Ziegler. There are a couple books already in the library on the Davis family, so will not spend a lot of time in that direction.

103

ON

THE

BANKS

OF

THE

MUSCATATUCK

Stories and Sketches and Historical notes on the maternal side of Wilbur Reynolds Family Including Ziegler, Arney, Davis, and Ziegler-Schneider families

ON THE BANKS OF THE MUSCATATUCK

HN: In 1902, screaming and kicking, a baby boy was born in his grandparents' house that set on a high promontory above the Muscatatuck. He was born with a crippled left hand and a partial left lung. His lovely mother was devastated, almost in a state of shock. His no nonsense grandmother, Sarah Catherine Arney Ziegler, grasped the situation and the child. "He will be a fine, strong man. You will see." And she saw to it. She and his grandfather, Charles, never allowed him to consider himself a cripple, and he grew up learning to do all the things a boy with two hands could do. It was his grandparents who raised him while his mother took the train every day to North Vernon to work. It was she who bought the little piece of land they lived on and in 1908, Charles built another house beside the little one. Lavina (Louvina) and Wilbur continued to live in the little house while Charles and Sarah lived in the larger house. That all changed when Lavina married Will Randall in 1914. She had divorced Wilbur's father, William Edwin

Reynolds, in 1904, for desertion. Edwin didn't want a crippled child and wanted his women and wine regardless of having a wife. That didn't set with Lavina, and she chose not to live like that. It took courage in 1904 to obtain a divorce, especially for a well brought up young lady. And she had been brought up right. Her greatest mistake in life was marrying the wrong man. I think all of Vernon must have known she was making a mistake when she married Edwin, but love is blind, at least until it dies, and in the face of abuse, love can die mighty quick.

Edwin was not content to ruin one woman life, and also in 1904 was run out of town when another fine young woman killed herself because he would not marry her. After she took the poison, (carbolic acid) she sent for him and he did come, although in a drunken state. He was too late.

However, Edwin's sad story is for another day. Let's get back to Lavina and Wilbur. Lavina (Louvina) worked during the week as a seamstress until her remarriage. On weekends, she taught Sunday School at the nearby Methodist church. She and Will Randall and his first wife had been friends for years. He had two boys when he started courting Vina. His wife had died just months before. His boys were Waldo and Ralph and Waldo was nine months older than Wilbur and Ralph a few months younger. When Will and Vina married, Sarah refused to let Wilbur go and live with his mother, so Wilbur moved into a small bedroom in his grandmother's house, a room whose window overlooked the lovely little town of Vernon. He visited from time to time the farm of his stepfather, a farm that lay outside Vernon by about three miles. The farm lay, as well, on the banks of the Muscatatuck near the Sullivan Ford bridge.

On the farm, Vina learned to be a farmer's wife. She had pigs to feed, geese, ducks, chickens and Guiana fowl. Oh yes, she had turkeys too. Days were busy. She was already thirty two years old, so she added to their family quickly. Earn was born in 1915; Elizabeth in 1916 and Stella in 1918.

Now, I have mentioned many details in this first story. All are true for Wilbur is my father and Vina my grandmother. The following stories are a mixture of fact and fiction. Most of the people mentioned are actual ancestors who settled in Jennings County. I may have misinterpreted their personalities but not the locations of the stories. These people lived on the banks of the streams of Jennings County. One could not live in that day and age without water for themselves and their livestock. So they built their cabins on the hills overlooking some stream, which provided water except in time of drought.

A river runs twisting and turning, through Jennings County, and there are many creeks. Jennings County is nestled in the low rolling hills of southern Indiana. The first stories take place on the Muscatatuck, where Vernon is found, encircled by three arms of the Muscatatuck, and where the Randall farm once prospered. It was also on the Muscatatuck that four Davis brothers and other Davis families settled in the early 1800s. Nathaniel Davis was Sarah's mother's grandfather, the father of Sarah who Sarah was named after. Sarah also married a Davis, her cousin, Charles. If you want to follow the family lines, there is a family chart at the beginning. The following sketches are word pictures of pioneer life, all resting on the streams my people settled on, names like Wyaloosing, Sand Creek, Wimple Creek, Crooked Creek, the Branch, Pleasant Run, Brush Creek and Graham Creek.

Loralyn Reynolds, 2012

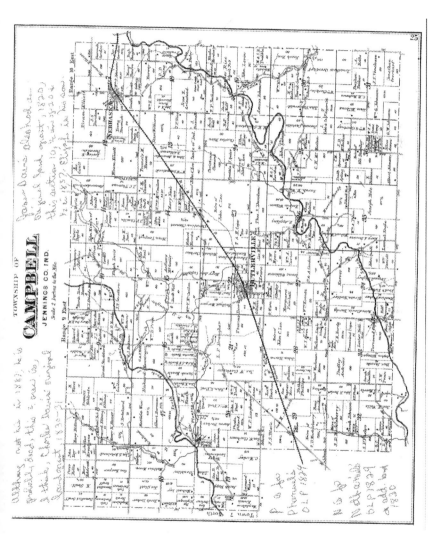

SNIPE HUNT

I chuckled quietly to myself where I lay hidden under the bed all warm and safe while my stepbrothers were sent back out into the cold and dark to hunt, yes, for me.

They had taken me snipe hunting, left me to hold the bag, and did not return as promised. It was the year after my mom had married their dad, and I was being tested. I had not visited the farm very often and was still considered a town kid. But I wasn't as dumb as they thought, and tonight would be an eye opener for them. We were respectively thirteen, twelve and eleven. I was in age in the middle.

They, of course, had come back for me when they thought I'd had long enough to have gotten good and scared. But of course, I wasn't there but the bag was. I had made my way back to the house in the growing darkness, and slipped into the house undetected, and hidden under the bed. After hunting for me in the surrounding woods, Waldo and Ralph had dragged themselves back to the house and confessed what they had done. They were sent back out not once but twice before I was found. We were all punished, but they were exhausted and although we played tricks on each other over the years, they never tried anything like that again.

In fact, it was my sixteen birthday before they came up with something so idiotic that it could have gotten one of them killed. That they lived to produce families and children who have done well in the world is living proof that idiocy does not necessary run in families.

This event occurred on the morning of my sixteenth birthday, December 17th, 1918. It was just before dawn. Snow lay on the ground, covering wooded hills and open pastures of the farm on the Muscatatuck that belonged to my stepdad. Waldo, Ralph and I all slept in the same bed in a little room separated from the main house. We had our own wood heating stove, but it was still mighty cold. We slept with quilts piled high and as was our habit, we all slept naked. I was in the middle that night, and I was sleeping on my stomach. I must add here that we kept a loaded shotgun sitting by the door. We did not usually keep a piece of lumber in the room and one of the other boys must have brought it in and hidden it. As you now have probably guessed, I was in store for a birthday spanking.

As darkness was pushed away by the coming light of morning, and a grayness permeated the land, Waldo and Ralph snuck out of bed. They stirred the fire in the small pot bellied stove in order to give themselves some light. The boys proceeded to position themselves. Waldo picked up the wooden plank board. Ralph got ready to pull off the covers. With perfect timing, the birthday spanking was administrated, one jerk of the quilts, one sound wop of the board applied to my backside. Their laughter was drowned in my actions. I came out of the bed, cursing them and grabbing the gun in one single motion. "I'll kill you," I shouted. They evidently did not expect that much fury from me, but they should have. They did not wait to see if I would really shoot them, for I am certain they were sure at that point that I would have. They were out of the door and must have run faster than they ever had, because as I have already told you, they lived to raise families. I followed for a long time before I cooled down and returned to the house, three half grown boys, butt naked running over those snow covered hills. Since the days the Indians had ruled that waterway, I have a feeling that those hills had not seen such a sight.

Wilbur A Reynolds
(As told to his children, 1960)

COMING TO INDIANA

It was December and the morning was cold. The horse thudded dully along through the morning grayness. The man tried to pull his coat closer about his neck. The coldness had already seeped through his woolen pants and long woolen underwear and the two pairs of socks he wore inside his boots.

Then it came! He merely glanced toward the east and there it was. The spender of a spectacular sunrise on a frost covered world. Rays of rose beginning to creep into a dull gray sky, touching the frost like a candle set in a winter window.

And the moment lent a lifting to his spirits and a difference to his day.

Nathaniel Davis, 1807

WHEN ALL IS SAID AND DONE

The wind howled like a banshee around the sturdy log cabin here in the Indiana wilderness. The fire in the fireplace snapped and crackled, lending both warmth and light to the room. Several gathered around the bed in the far corner where Margaret Murley Davis lay dying. The cabin was crowded with people. But my eyes were not on them. The others were being comforted by the quiet prayers of a man of God who stood with those around the bed. My eyes were on my brother, Nathaniel sitting before the fire, his mind far away from this scene, maybe back to the moment when he first laid eyes on Margaret Murley. Even now I can hear him tell the story, as he has told it a hundred times through the years.

"There I was, a half grown boy, rolling around on the ground with the Murley boys. We'd been sent over to the Murleys by our dad to help out with some wood chopping, and it had gotten off to a bad start. They'd said something about us just coming from Virginia, and being soft, and one word led to another, and there we were, rolling around and wrestling on that cold, frosty ground like fools. There was a shot rung out, and we all got mighty still. Then there in front of me was the prettiest girl I'd ever seen and she was holding a rifle on all of us. Her hair was the color of dark sand and it fell around her shoulders in waves. Her eyes were glinting blue and angry and her face was masked with disgust. She stood fine and proud like a young sapling and her words ripped us apart. She said, "Pa left me in charge and in charge I am. I expect all five of you worthless excuses of human beings to be back at work before I count to three, and if you're not, you'll be limping for the rest of your life." You can bet we were all on our feet in a split second, and back to work, all disagreements forgotten. And even though I wasn't yet a man, I knew I'd marry Margaret 'Peggy' Murley and I did."

Phanuel Davis, March of 1845

(Historical point: Most Davis researchers agree that Margaret Murley Davis died in 1845. Most agree that Nathaniel died in 1843 but some having him live up to 1880. So this scene may not be historical plausible, but it is the way I pictured it, so it is the way I wrote it. Nathaniel and Phanuel were definitely brothers and homesteaded on the Muscatatuck before 1820 where Pleasant Run runs into the Muscatatuck. The Davis men built their cabins in a similar style, two stories with a covered front porch. They likely all helped each other with the raising of their cabins. Several Davis men came to that part of Jennings County about the same time, all related but some of the connections are fuzzy. There was Nathaniel and Phanuel, definitely brothers, an Elijah and James near the same age as the brothers, and a Charles, William and Jonathan who were younger. There was also a Walter who had extensive household goods, did not show up in the 1820 census but bought land in 1820 near James, died shortly after. At his sale, several Davis men bought items.

The Davis families were from Virginia. They stopped for awhile in Kentucky. Margaret Murley was born in Kentucky during the time Daniel Boone and Harrod and Logan established their forts and held Kentucky for later settlement, making her family among those who dared more and risked more. There is no indication in the paperwork and census records of slaves being owned by the Davis families, but it can't be ruled out. There are plenty of curly haired people in that line, but a lot of those curls are red. After Nathaniel and Margaret married, we find some of their children born in Kentucky and some in Indiana. Sally (Sarah) was said to have been born en route to Indiana. Phanuel sojourned a bit in Ohio before arriving in Indiana.).

ALONG THE BANKS OF PLEASANT RUN

She was standing with the wet January snow falling about her, a lone figure silhouetted against the darkening sky. Across her shoulders was draped a well worn woolen cloak of gray that fell to her knees and around her neck was wrapped a long woolen scarf of rust that also covered her ears and chin. Her long hair of dark gold hung loose over her shoulders. She faced the grove of cedars to the south and the cabin lay behind her. The cabin was a sturdy, two story log structure built like all the Davis cabins here in this Indiana wilderness. The year was 1823. She was seventeen years old, and Charles Davis had come to claim his bride. She did not remember the day she had not loved her cousin, Virginia born Charles Davis, ten years her senior. She first remembered him when she was five years old and he had visited their home and she had sat on his knee by the fire while he had talked with her parents. He had run her silken curls through his strong young fingers while apparently absorbed in the adult conversation. He had also at other moments knelt with her before the fireplace and played with clay marbles, showing her how to shoot straight if that were possible on the puncheon floor. He had also held with her a lengthy conversation concerning her newest doll, whom she had named Dicyann, after the stories of their ancestor who had come alone to America and had been indentured to a Davis family. One of those Davis boys in that family in time become her husband. Her father had made the cornhusk doll for her for Christmas and her mother had dressed her with scraps from her recent sewing. Some day she would have her own live baby girl and she would carry the name Diantha or Dicy Ann and that real Dicy would mother ten children and have many, many descendents. But of course, Sarah knew none of this as she stood reflecting on her life and happiness to this point.

She had been a bride for a month now. She and Charles had been married December 19 of 1822 by Mr. John Vawter himself, the man who founded the town of Vernon. Of course the Vawters and Davis families had known each for some time, both had been in Kentucky and then to Indiana near the Ohio and then on to Jennings. She and Charles were still living with her parents, but Charles was looking for a small farm that would be nearby.

As she stood watching the snow fringe lace on the cedars, she reflected on her love. Charles had waited for her. He was twenty seven, past the time when most men marry, but he had worked and saved his money and waited for her to grow up. Now she was a grown woman, ready to make a home for her man and face together whatever lay before them. Sally (Sarah) Davis, January of 1823

ALONG THE BANKS OF CROOKED CREEK

She was the oldest daughter of Isaac and Diantha Davis Arney, but not their oldest child nor their oldest daughter. Both her parents had children before their marriage, her brother Bryon to her mother and her sisters Louisa and Charlotte, to her father by his first wife, Nancy, who died with one of the many fevers that assaulted the early settlers. Sarah Catherine, named after her beloved grandmother, Sarah Davis Davis, was a quiet, well behaved child who mothered her eight siblings. She caught the eye of Charles Ziegler who lived on Grayford Road, but Charles' mother discouraged Charles' attraction to Sarah because the Arney's were not land owners. On Crooked Creek, her father farmed for another man, and they were really poor.

But love overcomes all, and in 1881, April 6 to be precise, right before her April 10 birthday where she turned twenty two, she married Charles Ziegler. It was a love match of mutual commitment to the end of their days. They raised only two children, Lavina and Edward. Sarah did not want the large family her mother had, but she helped raise nieces and nephews and her grandson in the house Charles built for her at Vernon. From an upper bedroom window, one can see the entire town of Vernon.

Into her seventies, she chopped wood for her fire, made rag rugs on her loom, and remained in the house in Vernon. From time to time, Wilbur would come back to live with her. His bedroom was the one with the window toward the town. Her son, Edward, had no children of his own. His nephew, Wilbur, was the nearest to a son he could claim. Ed worked at the water plant in North Vernon. He did marry late in life.

Sarah Arney Ziegler

A WOMAN OF INTEGRITY

The sun was rising higher, gently flooding the pastures and fields. It was a lovely spring morning, and she paused from her washing and walked to the back of the house. Her eyes swept over the pig lot to cows grazing on the slope and beyond them the tree fringed hills. And just beyond that the Muscatatuck curved. The trees were covered with little leaves and her yellow Easter flowers were blooming. Soon the peony bushes would follow and then the hollyhocks that lined the path to the outside necessary. The scene before was peaceful and so was the one that played out in her mind, a spring and summer of blooming flowers planted with her own hands, and days filled with caring for a husband and three healthy little ones. Peace enveloped her and thankfulness welled up within her. She was a fortunate woman, she thought. She finally had a man who cared about her and their children, who worked hard all day and came home to her at night, and usually for his noonday meal as well. She had come to love the farm and loved being a farmer's wife. Yes, the work was hard but satisfying. And what more could anyone want from life than to have satisfying work and someone to love.

Lavina Ziegler Randall, April of 1925

Jim and Sally Conway described integrity as a basic acceptance of one's life as appropriate and meaningful. I believe it was at the above stage of her (my grandmother) life that she came to that and retained that attitude throughout most of her life. She raised a family that cares about each even unto the third and fourth generation. She was a wonderful grandmother, and I believe that what made her a great woman was what she had learned in the learning years of life. She had somehow found out who she was and learned to accept her strengths and weaknesses and in acceptance, had found she liked herself and could live happily with who she was. The best gift we can give to our family and friends is to learn to live happily with ourselves. I believe she had learnt that there are things you can live without and with and following, there are things you can't live without and with. I believe she had learned that you can live without fame and riches and worldly success, but you can't live without faith and love and hope and relationships. She had learned you can live with failure and disappointment and discouragement if you can pick up and go on. She came to know, too, that what you can't live with is anger and bitterness and resentment or an unforgiving spirit, either in yourself or others. I am also assured that her relationship with God was the most important relationship of her life and in that relationship she learned all the really important things in life—loving, giving, forgiving, hoping, enduring, believing and accepting and being accepted. She was a woman of inner integrity.

(I would like to think her daughters and granddaughters have worked, are working to be that kind of woman. IN the last few years, we girl cousins have been getting together two or three times a year in order to share more deeply. We have had some rich experiences and come to appreciate each other on a deeper level. I see my grandmother more and more in these lovely women. We are far from perfect but as we laugh, love and share (and eat), I believe we understand and appreciate each other more, bond at a deeper level, support and, yes, are becoming more like our grandmother.)

Loralyn Reynolds, 'Tribute to my Grandmother'

HN: Grandma's farm life included the keeping of geese, turkeys, chickens, and other fowl. She stole feathers and down from the geese for pillows and for sale. She also would dress out any of her fowl for sale to a specific customer. The typical day started before five o'clock. She would have breakfast on the table by then, sliced bread or biscuits, fried bacon or sausage, or pancakes. Bread making was sourdough, about every third day. Besides watching three little kids, she cooked, baked, sewed, cleaned, tended the chickens and her other fowl, gathered eggs, planted flowers, gardened, canned and preserved. She also rescued kids off the barn roof, fried up their favorite snack of baby pigeons which the children had gathered by climbing the silo. She also would have Pearl hitched up to the buggy and taking three little kids, would drive into Vernon for shopping, perhaps taking in feathers, or eggs or home churned butter for trade at the store. Sometimes they took the buggy for fun excursions. Aunt Elizabeth told the story of one such excursion on her brother, Earn's birthday, June 14th. It was a warm day and they put on their swim suits and went swimming. Then suddenly in the afternoon, the day turned cold and as they hurried to return home, they were actually snowed on. She couldn't remember what year that occurred.

DIANTHA ON CROOKED CREEK

HN: My grandmother, Louvina Ziegler Reynolds Randall, stated that her grandmother, Diantha Davis Arney, was one of the many women forced to cook for Morgan's raiders when they passed through in 1863 during the Civil War. It would have been her one claim to fame. In love and engaged to James Gatewood, she gave birth to a son in 1849 at the age of seventeen. Gatewood had left and never returned for her. Her marriage to Isaac Arney was one of hard work, baby after baby, and poverty. She had the dark red hair common to the Davis family. She was the mother of ten children and step mother to two. There is a section of this book with more information on the Arney and Davis families. Loralyn Reynolds, 2014

From the Banks of the Muscatatuck to Wimple Creek
(Elizabeth Louise Randall Robbins)

She was born on the Randall farm on the Muscatatuck on the last day in July of 1916. She was the first daughter of Louvina Ziegler and Will Randall who already shared a son, Ernest. Will had brought two other sons, Waldo and Ralph, and Louvina one son, Wilbur Reynolds, to their 1914 marriage. So Elizabeth had four big brothers to adore her. Her favorite childhood memories include playing with her brothers and sisters, in the woods and fields and boating on the river, climbing the walls of the silo for pigeons, buggy rides to Vernon with her siblings, her mother driving old Pearl, and sitting beside her mother on the organ bench with her sister, Stella, on the other side, while her mother played and they sang songs together. She went to school at Vernon and finished at the high school there in 1934. She had attracted an upperclassman early in her HS years and two months after her graduation, she married him, on her eighteen birthday. Their first child, Charles William "Bill" was born in 1937 and then they lost a daughter, Donna, before the birth of Karen in 1943. It was that year they moved into the house Archie had built for her on Wimple Creek in Sand Creek Township, across from the old Wimple Creek School house that Archie had attended as a boy. She raised her family there, (including Patricia born in 1948), canned and quilted, sewed, and gardened, cooked and cleaned and sit by Archie in that house where he died in 1993. She and Archie were very supportive of their family, their extended family, their friends, community and church. Archie farmed and ran a sawmill. (His brother-in law, Wilbur, worked for him from 1947 to 1967). Both Archie and Elizabeth taught Sunday School in their church at Pleasant View and later were active members of the North Vernon Christian Church. Elizabeth was a 4H leader for many years and worked at Gumbles, Regal Rugs and the License Branch. When her mother aged she and Archie put a trailer on their property and checked on Vina every day. She loved to cut hair and often cut hair for family and friends and gave perms. One niece's fondest memory at Aunt Elizabeth's was having a perm there on a summer day, being teased by Uncle Archie about the bad smell, having lunch with all of them, and having Aunt Elizabeth take a picture of the three girls (Karen, Loralyn and Patty) standing in front of the house frowning at the sun. Of course, nieces and nephews were there often, but not often enough, because one of Uncle Archie's nephews and one of Aunt Elizabeth's nieces found themselves dating and horrified to discover they both had the same Uncle Archie and Aunt Elizabeth. It turned out to be OK when upon more communication they found that they were not cousins and have been happily married for forty some years.

Archie and Elizabeth's marriage covered almost sixty years. No one who knew them would doubt their love and commitment to each other but they didn't always agree on everything and were probably equally stubborn but when it came to the really important issues, they were there for each other. Their union survived and endured throughout the losses of two daughters (Karen in an accident at age twenty-two), the losses of two of Elizabeth's brothers, their parents, a grandchild and a fire at the mill. There were lean years and more profitable years, good years and better years, health issues and sometimes tough decisions to be made, but throughout it all their love for each other grew and their faith in God. They both have left a legacy of love and faith to their family.

I hope I have not painted a picture of a super saint, but of a loving, caring woman who loved and loves her family, who despite her few faults, was and is committed to her family, and to her God, and who always strove to "do all things well".

Other Memories

One of the joys of doing family research is the people you meet, yes, cousins, but often removed by several generations, but there is still a bond there. A common ancestor is your connection. In the late 90s, Jim Davis and his lovely wife vacationed to Indiana from Colorado in order to do Davis research. We had been communicating by mail and they just showed up and called. I spent as much time as with them as I could. We visited the Brush Creek Cemetery where so many Davis people are buried but other cemeteries as well that hold Davis relatives, such as Butlerville and Vernon. Also we visited the sites of original homesteads like Phanuel and Nathaniel's on the Muscatatuck and James Davis' as well. His is the only one still owned by Davis descendents. The Colorado James is a descendent of Nathaniel Davis. They were a delightful couple and we stayed in touch until Jim's death a few years later.

Another pleasant surprise occurred when one of my favorite secretaries at Muscatatuck, Karen Bolin, and I discovered that we were distant cousins. One of us mentioned having family buried at Brush Creek and the other said, "so do I". She is a descendent of James Davis. For the reference of others who do not know Jennings County, the Brush Creek Cemetery is located behind the Urban Training Center on what is referred to as Camp Holland road. This is in Campbell township east of North Vernon.

But closer in blood and family ties are memories of family times on the banks of the Muscatatuck. As a child, the family often got together at Uncle Waldo's, whose farm was on the Muscatatuck with a branch running through the farm that emptied into the river. In recent years, the cousins have gotten together for lively lunches at Sue's, his daughter's whose home sets on that same property. Also family gatherings were often at Jo Ann's, Uncle Waldo's other daughter, who has a home in

Vernon, which of course, is on the Muscatatuck. And then as a child, there were those special visits to Grandma's house, which was in Vernon, just across from the Courthouse. We played Dominos and other games. Grandma always kept toys for children to play with. We were also treated to spicy cookies from her cookie jar. Once I helped her make watermelon rind preserves. Then there are also special memories of good times at Aunt Stella's when I was a child. She also then lived at Vernon.

Life at the mill included not only our getting to play in the sandbox under the apple tree, but sometimes when the mill was shut down, we got to play in the sawdust piles. There was also a pond for fishing, and there was also always a dog. Aunt Elizabeth gave me perms, cut my hair, taught me to cook and bake, and tried to teach me to sew. She was less successful with that but she did try. She also sewed for me and loved me as one of her own. Uncle Archie gave me my first Bible and told me to read it every day. I did that for a long time, and regret that I am not so faithful now.

There were always flowers at their house, and I've tried to plant flowers everywhere I go. That has been a lot of places. Once I had managed to plant some flowers, and just a few came up. We had friends over for lunch and their little boy pulled up everyone. I was devastated but tried to make light of the situation. Now I can laugh about it. But my grandmother and Aunt Elizabeth and I loved colors and patterns, thusly flowers, and then quilts.

And finishing up this section, I must mention that the Randall-Reynolds reunion was held at the Muscatatuck County Park in August of each year, and of course the park is on the Muscatatuck. It is now held elsewhere, so if you're attending, call for place and directions.

Loralyn Reynolds, 2012

Margaret Murley Reflects

With unhurried motions, she prepared the simple supper meal, corn pone and venison stew with dried herbs from her own herb garden. She was an old woman now and only she and Nathaniel were left in the two storied log cabin built high above Pleasant Run and the Muscatatuck River. There had been thirteen children at one time in this cabin. Then the older ones started leaving, building cabins of their own. Now they had all left. But most lived near, near enough to see often.

She cooked by the light of the fireplace and the little of winter light that filtered through the windows. Not all cabins built in the Indiana wilderness in these early days had windows but Davis cabins did, were always two storied and a roofed porch to shade you when you sat shelling beans or in the cool of evening, just chewing the fat, or to be quiet and listen to the evening bird serenade.

They had come to Indiana in 1806. Her Sallie had been born in Kentucky in 1805 on their way to Indiana. They had not reached Indiana until 1806 and then had lived a couple places just north of the Ohio River, until Nathaniel and his brothers and cousins decided on the new county of Jennings. The lay of the land reminded them of Virginia where they had been born and raised.

She, however, had been born in Kentucky in 1778, near the Lexington Station. Daniel Murley had taught all his children to shoot straight, ride tall and bow to no man. As a girl, she could shoot straighter, ride faster, and fight dirtier than any of her brothers. The only man she'd ever bowed to was Nathaniel Davis, and that was just a curtsy when he had asked her to dance. He couldn't shoot as well as she could, but he did ride taller and he danced beautifully. He had set his sights for her years before. They were married in 1800 and wasted no time in producing babies.

Finally, with supper waiting, Peggy lit a candle. It was total darkness out now, no more sign of the rose tinted sky against a canopy of blues and gray.

Nathaniel would be home soon. He was talkin' about moving once again. She hoped he would realize they were too old. Phanuel, his brother, who lived on the farm across from them (the Pleasasnt Run Creek ran between the farms) was not interested in leaving. Maybe that would hold him.

Margaret 'Peggy' Murley Davis

MURLEY

HN: Margaret "Peggy" Murley, the wife of Nathaniel Davis was born in Kentucky during its most tumultuous time. Her father, we think was Daniel Murley, born 1744 in Augusta County, Virginia, married a Margaret in 1781 (?)
in Greenbrier, VA, and in that same year ventured to Kentucky where a daughter carrying her mother's name was born.

Kentucky was still a battleground at this time. The first influx of settlers was in 1775, 1776 after Dunmore's War. By 1777, those alive and there were few, decided on the whole to leave. There were only 103 able bodied men in February of 1777 at the two Kentucky settlements still inhabited, Harrodsburg and Boonesboro. But in 1779, there was a resurgence of settlers. They built new forts and established new settlements, including the Lexington settlement by a man named Patterson. It was against this backdrop that Margaret Murley was born in 1781 near Lexington.

Margaret's parents were either very foolish or very courageous to venture into Kentucky at this time. Historians state that it was only the very foolish or the very courageous that were found there at the time, and the fools all died but so did most of the courageous.

It is believed Margaret grandfather was also Daniel Murley, born 1728 in Chester Co. PA and died in Augusta Co, VA in 1755. His wife's name was Judith. The next generation was Cornelius Murley, born 1707 in Ireland, and died in Augusta Co. VA. Cornelius Murley was described of dark complexion, thick set man with bushy black hair, held a grim look. He was come into the mountainous part of the country with Col James Patton and into the Shenandoah Valley of Virginia around 1740.

He must have been indentured, because we get the description from a newspaper, the Gazette, wherein Patton is trying to resecure his servant, describing him as an Irish servant man wearing a blackish Kersey coat with a patch on one sleeve, about 35 years old, also wearing and old hat, trousers and shoes with latchets. 40 Shillings were offered for his return. The year was 1742. Cornelius Murley was also described as a brawler. Murley researchers believe both Murley and Patton and Murley's son Daniel died during an Indian raid at Greenbrier in 1755.

Margaret had a brother, William Murley, born 1776 in VA and died in 1831 in Cumberland CO, KY.
(This would explain why Nathaniel and Margaret named a first son, William, and even though William was a common name for Davis sons, it would have been reinforced by Margaret.)

*The above information is from a website of a Murley/Davis researcher and assorted historical texts.
The description of Murley's bushy black hair reinforces the possibility that this is our ancestor. Several cousins I have met from the Davis—Murley line have this kind of hair.

Who were They? Davis Family History

It was a hard time and a hard life, but life is always hard, or at least that is the way I think of it after all this time. That does not mean that there is not laughter, and love and loyalty but loss is a portion for any man, and the generations of my family have affirmed that.

They came from Virginia to Kentucky and then on to Indiana. Many of my line stayed, but many of the Davis families moved on to Illinois, to Iowa, to Kansas, and on and on.

Several Davis families, all somewhat related, came to southern Indiana between 1802 and 1825 and many of these ended up in Jennings County by the time of the 1820 census. A newspaper article determines that James with son Addison came to claim their farm in 1820, hacking their way through tangled growth and trees to reach their claim southeast of Vernon. Of course, it was on a creek, Brush Creek and near the Muscatatuck River. Davis men did three things consistently. They settled near waterways; they built two story cabins with covered front porches, and they fathered large families.

There are many Davis researches and many family documents that don't agree, but are obviously talking about the same family, so it isn't the easiest of families to research, so I take the advice of a long forgotten comrade, who said, "It is your story! Write it your way." So here is my version. I know Nathaniel Davis was my great great great great grandfather. His daughter, Sarah, Sallee", "Sally" was my paternal grandmothers' grandmother's mother. I am sure she married a relative, Charles Davis, several years her senior. He was born in Virginia, she in Kentucky. He was probably a first or second cousin, but as already stated; reliable family documents do not agree. Many insist he was a younger brother to Nathaniel and Phanuel, but that throws off the Sarah marrying her cousin???? (Unless, as the Davis intertwined in marriages, he was a half brother to Nathaniel and Phanuel and also a cousin. It is possible, but a little unusual).

Anyway, Jennings marriage records have Charles and Sarah marrying in 1822. Records show they had 14 children, but the youngest was their grandson, Byron, Diantha's woods colt child. There is documentation for this as well as my own grandmother's statement.   ·

We think we have a rather accurate list of the children, and some information on some of them. Also true of Nathaniel, Phanuel and James. These lists are included with this summary.

Trying to reach back another generation has been difficult. Davis researchers link these men to several different names. At this time, 2012, the favorite for Charles is a Charles William Davis, born to James (James was born in Wales, came to America (Maryland) and settled in Bedford CO., Virginia where his children were born including also a James, George and John; died 1819 in VA; was a Captain and fought from Hampshire Co. VA in the Revolutionary War.) James' sons and widow including Charles William, who was a widower, and his five children and his brothers, John, and George and their families migrated to Ross County, Ohio. Charles William remarried and perhaps Charles Michael did not like his stepmother because it seems only he, of that family, came to Indiana. Most likely the Davis family he married into were related. I still hold to the second cousin theory, but not hard and fast.

The second theory I now hold is that Elijah is the father of Nathaniel and Phanuel and maybe James, but there was also a brother named Elijah. Now we bring in Walter, who gave PA as his former home, was here per land in 1820, buying land next to James, died in early 1820's and left an estate that was auctioned by Edward Davis. That theory would also support the four Davis brothers coming from the south. That would mean the 'four' were not James, Nathaniel, Phanuel and Charles as put forth, but Elijah, Nathaniel, Phanuel and James. (A James, TT, and Ben were listed in 1807 census of Clark county, may or may not be a connection).

All the Davis men who came to Indiana claim to have been born in Virginia and probably were, but Virginia at that time also included what is now West Virginia, Kentucky, and part of Ohio. Such places as Amherst Co (Maybe Charles' birthplace); Wythe CO (Maybe Phanuel's birthplace) and Bedford Co, (already mentioned (as birthplace of Charles William), and Hampshire Co, from which James Davis fought as a Captain in the War of Revolution.

These places were all considered, at the time, a part of the Frontier, the mountainous areas of Virginia. There was still Indian trouble. If there is a connection, Amherst CO and Wythe Co are only 100 to 150 miles a part, not so very far for men who could walk 30 to 50 miles a day. Amherst and Bedford counties are adjoining and Hampshire Co is just below Maryland, (now in WV) and much farther from the other areas. Ross Co. Ohio is in the middle of the southern portion of that state.

SO my historical Davis sketches that follow are a combination of the known, the suspected, and historical information of the era. No apologies, no regrets, just utter relief that I only inherited their Welsh stubbornness, not the characteristic red, curly hair (but it looks great on all of you who have it).

Oh, let me add that Phanuel's researchers have pretty good documentation that he was born in VA, (1785) went to Madison CO., Ky., married there, (1807) had land, then went to Ohio (Clermont CO) (Brown CO) (child born there in 1818) and then to Jennings by 1820. (census) He fought in the war of 1812 from Ohio.

Nathaniel born in VA (1778), migrated to KY. Married Kentucky born Margaret Murley in Lexington around 1800, first children born in KY. Believe Sally was born in KY in 1805. Then it is uncertain. But seem to have gotten to Indiana at least 1813 where a child was born, first settled south of Jennings, maybe Jefferson A lot of Davis families stayed there, but Nathaniel was in Jennings by the 1820 census. He and Phanuel settled on Pleasant Run where it empties into the Muscatatuck. This is in Campbell Twp above Butlerville near the Urban Training Center.

As I have already stated, documentation shows that Charles and Sarah (Sally or Sallee) were married in Dec of 1822 in Jennings CO. We can only assume they lived with her parents for a while. In 1825, they bought land from Robert Elliot in what is today the town of Zenas in Columbia Twp. The old name of the town was Ely. They paid $20 and sold it for the same price in 1829 to James Butler. We do not know why they were at that spot at that time. We do know that the land Zenas occupies was an OLP by Stephen Beard in 1821.

Beard sold it to David Elliot in Dec of 1824. Elliot did not plat the town of Zenas until 1837, but there was likely a settlement there of sorts when Charles and Sarah moved there. Their place was a portion of 24, 8, 9 (southeastern part of southwestern quarter) which is the area roughly where Leatherwood Creek empties into the Muscatatuck. This would be consistent with the way the Davis men chose their land. Anyway, Charles and Sarah would have had two little boys when they first bought the place and would have had two more children when they sold that acreage or lot, whatever it was, and moved to the 80 acres in Campbell Township where they remained until the1860s (Sarah died in 1864) (Charles sold 40 acres of his land in September, following her death, to Ephraim Hutton who was married to a Davis cousin, James' daughter, Rachel). There where Brush Creek empties into the Muscatatuck, (9,7,9, E half of the SW qt) they had nine more children, raised a grandson, and were only a few short miles from her folks.

My great great grandmother, their daughter, Diantha, (Dicey) was born in 1830 or 32. She was engaged to a Gatewood but he left her carrying his child and unmarried. She was seventeen years old. IN 1857, she married widower, Isaac Arney, who had two little girls. (Nancy and Charlotte). They had their own little girl in April of 1859, my great grandmother, Sarah (named after her grandmother) Catherine Arney. She became the Matriarch of the family, her younger brother and sisters often living with her family after she married Charles Ziegler in 1881. Diantha had lots of red curly hair and I have a picture of her. My grandmother looked a lot like her but didn't have the red hair. I believe my great grandmother, Sarah looked a lot like her grandmother, Sarah. Anyway, Isaac and Diantha had eight more children after the birth of Sarah. They finally started having boys. The first was Charles Arney. The second son was William O. Arney. There is a separate write up on the Arneys and Fogas if you wish to refer to it. The Fogas were also a large family, a branch of this Arney family, specifically the descendents of William O. Arney's daughter, Sophia, and Jacob Foga. Many remain in the area. One was in my high school class. One worked with my mother at Regals. I worked with one at MSDC. They are everywhere.

It is confirmed that James and Charles Davis and their wives are buried in the Brush Creek Cemetery. All have stones. There was at one time, a Baptist church there built of stone in 1860 (the log church was built in 1836). James either gave or sold the land for both and a school. Phanuel is supposedly buried in the Parker Cemetery in the wooded area across the road from his farm. Some researchers say Nathaniel moved west with some of his family before his death. Others say he died in 1835 and is buried in Jennings CO. Who knows????? He is last listed or mentioned in the 1830 census. Last land transaction I found was 1838. One researcher's death date is 1843 with Margaret dying in 1845.

Now how did they pay for their land?? There were several possibilities. There were several homestead acts; one (1800) allowed a man to buy as little as 40 acres at a $1.25 an acre and gave him so many years to pay it off. Those who had fought in some war were often entitled to military warrants, specifically allotted according to rank. The Homestead Act of 1862 provided 160 A., no other cost but the filing fee.

The items listed for sale at Walter Davis' sale were impressive, indicating a man more prosperous than the average 'pioneer pusher'.

If a Davis family researcher is researching Jennings County Davis families, he or she will most likely find them related if their branch came in the early 1800s. Two distinct families that don't seem to fit are the family of Septimus Davis who settled in the southern part of the county away from the others who spread out over Columbia and Campbell townships, and the family of William T. Davis who married Rosa Jones and settled near Brewersville in Sand Creek Township. I have an obit. On W. T. and he was born VA and there is a William listed as a grandfather, but other than that, he doesn't seem to fit. I find him of interest because I think his wife is a sister to my g-g-g grandmother, Amelia Jones who married WF Cheever.

*I have found the Davis research fascinating, but non-conclusive. SO I am going to leave it as is. I may never be assured who the next generation is beyond James, Charles, Phanuel and Nathaniel or what the exact relationship was. I am relatively confident that Phanuel and Nathaniel were brothers. Their descendents confirm this and they homesteaded next to each other. I am sure both James and Charles are related to them, but exactly how is a question mark to me. I am sure someone or other in the family fought in the Revolutionary War, but I am not sure who. There were so many Davis soldiers. It is impossible to pin it down without more to go on than I have. It would have been neat o to have found when my branch of the Davis family came to America and when and on what ship, but I know they've been here over 200 years and probably much, much longer.

*If anyone is researching this family and wants to look at my research, I am more than willing to share. The librarian knows how to get a hold of me.

Loralyn Reynolds

{Daughter of Wilbur Reynolds, granddaughter of Lavina Ziegler Reynolds Randall, great granddaughter of Sarah Arney Ziegler, and great-great granddaughter of Diantha Davis Arney, and great-great-great granddaughter of Sarah and Charles Davis, and gggg gd of Nathaniel and Margaret Murley Davis. (This 5ᵗʰ day of September of 2012)}

Davis Family Charts
(somewhat accurate)

Nathaniel Davis Married Margaret Murley in or near Lexington, Kentucky @ 1800
Born April 17, 1778 in Virginia
Died Year uncertain as is where
Father Name uncertain (My best guess based on research-Elijah)

Children

William	Born KY	1801
Joshua	"	1802
Daniel	"	1804
Sarah	"	1805
Alsey	"?	1807
Elijah	" "	1809
Elisha	" "	1810
Hiram	" IN	1813
Esquire	" IN	1815
Nathaniel	" "	1817
Samanthy	" "	1818
Noble F.	" "	1821
Lewis Byram	" "	1822

Phanuel Davis Married Jane Woods May 7, 1807 in Madison CO Ky.
Born January 6, 1785, Wythe CO, Virginia
Died March 28, 1864, Burial Parker Cemetery, Campbell Twp, Jennings County, IN

Children

Ruth	BornKY	1808
Joseph	OH	1811
Sarah	OH	1814
Mary (Polly)	OH	1816
Nathan	OH	1818
Ebenezer	IN	1820
Jane	IN	1823
Phanuel	IN	1826
John Calvin	"	1828
Harriet	"	1833
Luther	"	1838
Richard Waters	"	1838
(adopted)		

HN: Most of my information on Phanuel and much on Nathaniel came from Flo Miller. She is a great great granddaughter of Phanuel through his son, Ebenezer, who married Bridget McCalpin in Jennings CO and remained there. She confirmed where the two farms of these two Davis brothers lie, on either side of Pleasant Run as it empties into the Muscatatuck, Section 20 in Campbell Township. It lies on one of the back roads leaving the Muscatatuck Training Center. County Road 300 E. She actually visited the ruins of the log cabin Phanuel built on his farm and the cemetery across the road where Ebenezer is buried and his sister Harriet, and her husband, Aaron Parker. In the 1990s when I visited the spot, I could not find the cemetery, but did find remains of the stone fence Flo talked about and the stone bridge that crossed Pleasant Run. FLO stated that her family history confirms that Phanuel and Nathaniel were brothers and she is sure the others in the area at the same time were related, but is unsure if any of the others were brothers or cousins or uncle/nephew relationship.

Flo has a book on Davis history in the Jennings Co. library. There are some things I now do not agree with because of my own research, but the book and correspondence with her has helped me greatly. We never got to meet but tried several times. It just never worked out.

I am also including info on James Davis who was most definitely related. I believe he was a cousin to Nathaniel and Phanuel but many think he was a brother.

James Davis, Married Mary Ann October 25, 1802
Born 1772, Virginia
Died March 19, 1857 in Jennings County
Burial Brush Creek Cemetery

Children:	Elizabeth Davis 1803	John Davis 1808
	Mary Davis 1805	Addison Davis 1810
	William Davis 1813	Henry T. Davis 1816
	Elisha Davis 1819	Elijah Davis 1822

*Information on James comes from Joan Piercefield, Indianapolis, Indiana. She is a great-great-great great granddaughter of James connected by his son Addison through his daughter, Nancy who married an Ackerman.

According to Joan, family stories passed down include one that states we are shirt tail kin to Jefferson Davis. We are also related to Garfield, the Cat.

POSSIBLE LINKS: From the Calderon-Jones web site: States that Nathaniel's father was Elijah and his wife's name was Sarah. Also indicates a brother to Nathaniel named Elijah. And mentions a sister of Margaret Murley's named Charity. Charles and Sarah named a daughter Charity, younger sister to Diantha.

Census records indicate that there was a Sarah Davis, who settled in Clark County, Indiana around 1807. Was this Elijah's wife waiting for him to catch up? In the 1820 census, Nathaniel, Phanuel, James and an Elijah are all listed as being in Jennings, living near each other. This Elijah is over 45 years, possible brother or father.

Charles Davis Married Sarah 'Sally' Davis on December 19, 1822
Born November 26, 1795 in Virginia
Died September 26, 1871 in Jennings County, Indiana

Burial Brush Creek Cemetery

Children		
	Nehimiah 1823	Hiram Nathaniel 1825
	William Benjamin 1827	Rebecca 1829
	Amanda 1830	Diantha 1832
	Polly Ann 1833	Daniel 1834
	Charity 1835	Patsy C. 1837
	Francis M 1840	John W. 1842
	Alcy C 1847	Lewis Bryan 1849 (grandson)

Lewis Bryan is Diantha's son. He is buried beside his mother at Vernon. He fought in the Civil War. As mentioned before, Diantha married a widower, Isaac Arney in 1857. He already had two little girls, Louisa and Charlotte. (Charlotte married a Bush) Isaac and Diantha had nine children together, their first child together was born in 1859. THat was Sarah Catherine who married Charles Ziegler (See the following Ziegler history for more or the Arney Section. Charles and Sarah were my dad's grandparents).

The Davis family history indicates a people of faith. James gave land for church and school. So did Phanuel.

Know Right Now God is Touching You

Know right now
God is touching you!
He saw all this coming.
God is touching you.

Yes, God is touching you
Holding you in His arms
Giving you His peace
And a generous portion
Of His unfailing grace.

I want to say "I love you"
Because I really do
And know that I'm hurting
Right along with you.

It isn't what I would choose for you
Scrabble I'd rather play
And laugh with you
With a kettle of soup
On a snowy and cold day

But hope is what we cling to
And faith will see us through
And joy comes in the morning
His promise is so true!

Let his presence keep you
What else can you do?

A SHORT ZIEGLER—
SCHNEIDER HISTORY

I have not gotten very far in my research on this section of the family. My grandmother, Lavina (Louvina) Ziegler, my dad's mother, was the daughter of Charles Ziegler and Sarah Catherine Arney. Charles and Sarah were married April 6, 1881 in Jennings County. Sarah had been born in Jennings County on April 10, 1859, the daughter of Isaac Arney and Diantha Davis. She was one of twelve. Charles was born in Jefferson County in 1854, the son of Isaac Ziegler and Sarah Catherine Schneider. The family moved to Jennings County, Vernon Township in 1858, to a farm on Grayford Road. I honestly do not know whether Isaac built the log cabin they raised their family in or whether it was already standing. Isaac had been working on the railroad, from Madison to Vernon. My grandmother stated he was working on the railroad from Madison at the very start of its inception but I question that, because they didn't arrive in Indiana until the 1840s and came on a flatboat shortly after their marriage in Berks County, Pennsylvania, where they both had been born in 1821. They first settled in Madison and lost two children there. Then my great-grandfather, Charles was born in Madison in 1854. In 1858, they made the move to the farm on Grayford Road. (Isaac Ziegler from Manlove Butler; deed, Dec 28, 1858, W ½ N.E. 17,6,9; 80 acres). I do not know whether they moved into the log cabin already standing there or whether Isaac built it, but they raised their family of four children in that small cabin, a one room log cabin with a loft and a lean-to kitchen and small room off the side of the kitchen. I can describe it so well because it still stands, now on Highway Seven on the way between Vernon and Madison. Isaac bought more land later. Close neighbors were the Grimes family who had also come from Pennsylvania. One can speculate that they knew each other before. The two families were most definitely friends for several generations after their arrival in Indiana.

Years ago, I interviewed two of Isaac and Sarah's grandchildren who had lived near their grandparents as children, Minnie Powell, (mother of Bob, Bill and Betty Powell (Williams)) and Lizzie Parker. Minnie and

Lizzie and their brother, Walter, were the children of Henry and Rosa Ziegler Parker. Rosa was a sister to Charles. She and her husband farmed nearby. Rosa had three grand children and ten great grandchildren. Grandson Robert, (Bob) Powell had three sons, Richard, Ronnie and Steven. Grandson, William (Bill) Powell (married to Wendy) has a son and daughter, Dusty (Duke) and Catherine. Granddaughter, Betty, married Jim (Bud) Williams, has five sons, John, Allen, Mark, Bruce and Robert Williams. (Betty, born June of 1923, has become a personal friend and has helped me with my research. Her brother, Bob, was a principal when I started high school. It was he who told me I was related to him, and was always very kind).

Back to the interview: Lizzie said that her grandmother, Sarah, was a small woman but a little plumpish, a fastidious house keeper who used to give their beloved grandfather a frequent tongue lashing in German when he wouldn't wipe his boots after coming in from the barn. Isaac and Sarah's other children were Daniel and Chester. Daniel did marry late in life but left no children. Chester moved to Minnesota and has more descendents than any of his siblings. I saw a website on his Descendents. Our grandmother kept in touch with his daughter until her own death. Chester's children were Leola (married McCormick), Sam, Frank and Lynn. Leola had a son, Wilfred, who lived in Indianapolis. She lived in Mora, Minnesota.

Rosa did leave descendents in Jennings County as mentioned above, and only through her daughter, Minnie. Walter married but there were no living children and Lizzie never married.

Isaac fell and broke his hip while doing chores the winter of 1901 and died shortly after from resultant pneumonia. (Interestingly, this is the same winter that our great-great grandfather Renn did the same thing in Sand Creek township.) It must have been a really bad winter. Probably the two men had never met even though their grandchildren married that year in November. Isaac and Sarah Catherine and Uncle Dan are all buried at Ebenezer Cemetery which was near their farm. Sarah lived until 1907, and Dan remained with her, hitching the old white horse, Bob, to the buggy and taking her to town when she got blue. The house still stands on Grayford Road that Uncle Dan spend the rest of his years in after he married Mrs. Bess Vinson. It was most likely a marriage of convenience.

Grandma Vina and Lizzie and Minnie gave me the names of some of Isaac's sisters and brothers. There was a Matilda who married a William Schneider, and a Polly who married a Sheridan (son Henry). Also a Harriet who had a son Henry and a daughter Sue, who married a Lickenhaley. There was a sister who married a Karst and had a daughter, Anna who married Peter Eckert. (I have a picture of the Eckert family taken May 13, 1940 at a family celebration.) The Eckerts lived in Huntington, Indiana. Isaac also had a brother named William. Sarah had a bother name John whose wife was Abba. I have other pictures from Pennsylvania. One is of William E. Sheridan, taken at Williamsport, PA. Another is from Muncy, PA and another from Lebanon. Evidently some of their siblings came also to Indiana and others stayed in Pennsylvania. Minnie and Lizzie also told me that the cousins from up north in Indiana would ride the train and come visit. Through the years the connections were lost.

I found Sarah Schneider Ziegler's death record. It states that her father's name was, I think, the spelling is Samuel. It is difficult to decode. It could be Samuel or David or Daniel. The letter looks like a D but looks like the S in the spelling of Sarah and Schneider. Her mother's name is given as Sarah Binder. And it is given that parents were both born in Pennsylvania. I did find a Samuel Snyder in the 1830, Berks County census, who would fit. The difference in spelling may mean nothing. It does indicate a child, a female between the ages of five and ten, which would fit our Sarah. All else it gives us is that the female in the house was between forty and fifty, the adult male between thirty and forty and four children, a male 15-20, a female 10-15, and a female and a male between 5-10. There is also a Daniel Snyder with a female child of the right age.

I did not get even that far for Isaac. The best I can do in the 1930 census is a John Zigler who had a male child of the right age. Without more documentation, I will not accept that. What seems more likely is taken from the 1850 census, a Daniel Zeigler, 49 with wife, Catherine, 48 and daughters, Lygeria, (I think this is Polly), 18, Catherine, 16, Harriet,

13, Matilda, 11, Caroline, 10, and sons, William, 14 and Daniel at 4. There were most likely older siblings which would include Isaac who had left home by this time. Please note that there are three firm matches, sisters Harriet, Matilda and brother, William. There is also the name Daniel used by both families. I vote for this ancestor. Record indicates that Daniel was born in Pennsylvania. He was a farmer.

Lizzie and Minnie tried to describe their grandfather for me. They were only children when he died. They said he was of medium height and sort of on the heavy side. We have no picture of him but one of Sarah when she was older, also one of Isaac's mother or maybe two.

Sometimes I see traits of Sarah Catherine Schneider in me, and when I do, I try to deal with them quickly. She appears to have been a sharp tongued woman but maybe it was just unhappiness finding its way to the surface. The family lore says she did not approve of Charles' choice of a wife, but that did not stop his marriage, and it seems to have been an unusually good match. Her reasons for disapproval most likely centered in the fact that the Arneys were poor, and did not own land. Sarah's father worked for another farmer. But Sarah Arney was not her parents. She refused to have the big family her parents had produced even though she always opened her home to her brothers and sisters in their bad times.

Sarah and Charles had two children, our grandmother, Louvina, born the 21st of January in 1882, and Edward born the next year. Edward married late in life and left no children. It began to look as if Charles and Sarah would not have many offspring after Lavina's first marriage ended in divorce and only one child who was born with a crippled hand. But in 1914 she remarried, a local man, who had two sons and had lost his wife to cancer. Lavina's son, Wilbur. was nine months younger than Waldo and fifteen months older than Ralph. Vina and Will Randall had three more children together, Earnest born June 14, 1915, Elizabeth, born July 31, 1916 and Stella Catherine, born March 13, 1918. These three children plus Wilbur gave Sarah and Charles numerous descendents. (Which will detail in a separate following section)

Charles died in June of 1915 after a short illness. His obituary follows:

Charles E Ziegler, good citizen and prominent Knight of Pythias died June 18, 1915, born North Madison, Jefferson County, Indiana on June 4, 1854, married April 6, 1881, was a kind, indulgent father and husband, united with the Ebenezer M. E. Church when a young man, having been christened in the German Lutheran Church. Has two living brothers, Daniel of Jennings County and Chester of Ogilvie, Minnesota and a living sister, Rosa Parker, also of Jennings County. Two brothers and one sister died in infancy.

He was a kind friend and good neighbor. He possessed great patience and anticipation for a speedy recovery of health. However, he expressed himself as ready to answer 'the call' and quietly fell asleep, aged 61 years and 14 days.

"Like leaves on trees the race of men are found, now green in youth, now withering on the ground. Another race the following spring supply. They fall successive and successive rise. So generations in their course decay. So flourish these when those have passed away."

Funeral was held by Rev Jann. Burial in Vernon Cemetery.

It is an unusual obituary, and lays the groundwork for the next generations. I know without a doubt my father loved him very much.

Charles' death occurred four days after the birth of his second grandson, Ernest. Probably Sarah had planned to help with the birthing, but needed to be at Charles' bedside. And our grandmother, Lavina, would not have been able to attend the funeral since she would have still been in childbirth recovery. Chances are that Charles never saw this grandchild. Sarah continued to live in the house he had built her in 1908. She lived until 1937, with Wilbur continuing to make his home with her. He had been only twelve at the time of his grandfather's death. The house is at the curve that goes into Vernon. Family lore says Charles Ziegler built both houses, that dad was born in the little house where the family was living at the time, and that Charles built the larger house later. Documentation is as follows. Newspaper clipping in 1908 says Charles Ziegler started a new house. Courthouse records state that $400.00 worth of improvements made on Lot 187 between 1907-1911. (There are two lots and two houses there, 187 & 186.) In 1902, when Dad was born, the house was owned by Robert Leavitt, and the 1900 census says Charles and Sarah were renting. Interestingly, the place changed hands several times quickly. Leavitt to Dole in 1903; Dole to Deversey in 1905 and in September of 1905, Deversey to Vina Reynolds. It was only in October of 1914, the month before her marriage to Will Randall, that Vina put it in Sarah's name. (Note: for some reason, never anything in Charles' name) It was sold four months after Sarah's death in June of 1937 to the Laymans, who kept it for quite a long time. The house is about to fall down and that is a shame. It is a very interesting house. It has downstairs a front parlor, a bedroom, a dining room and big kitchen. In one of these room, Sarah kept her loom. She created rag rugs for folks. There was a basement where Sarah chopped wood. The upstairs could be reached by a very narrow staircase. There were three bedrooms, my father's overlooked the town of Vernon. Out back was a hen house where Sarah kept chickens. Sarah had a goiter which was never removed. It was her joy to have her grandchildren stay with her. Aunt Elizabeth stayed with her often. Her son Ed lived with her a long time. He worked for the North Vernon Pump House or Water Works, was a second father to my dad.

Descendents of Charles and Sarah Catherine Arney Ziegler

(1) Son Edward Ziegler, born 1883 (no offspring)

(2) Daughter,(Birth spelling, Louvina) Lavina, born January 21, 1882

1899 Graduated from Vernon High School

1901 Married William Edwin Reynolds.

1902, December 17, gave birth to her first son, Wilbur Alvadore Reynolds. (See section on Wilbur Reynolds Family)

1904 Divorced William Edwin Reynolds on grounds of desertion

1914 Married Will Fisk Randall who had two sons

1915 June 14, gave birth to her second son, Ernest who married Lorinda Harmon in 1935, and had three children, (1936) Shirley; (1944) Linda; and (1947) Tom. Shirley has three sons and a daughter, Jesse, David, Mark and Valorie. Linda has three daughters, Pam, Melissa and Michelle, and Tom two sons, Jason and Joshua and a daughter, Jennifer.

1916 July 31, Vina gave birth to Elizabeth Randall who married Archie Robbins on her birthday in 1934, had four children, (1937) Charles William (Bill); (1943) Donna (who died in infancy); (1943) Karen and (1948) Patty. Bill has three children, Jeffery, Charla, and Cheryl and there was a daughter who lived only a few months. Karen was killed in an automobile accident in 1965 and left one son, Allen Miles. Patty has two children, Gregg and Amy Thompson.

1918 March 13, Vina gave birth to her final child and second daughter, Stella Catherine. Stella who married Frank Fisher July 25, 1936 and has three children, (1939) James Edward (Jim,) who has two children; (1941) Ida, who has one son, Steve Harding; and (1942) Robert (Bob), who has one son, Jeffery Fisher. After Frank's death, Stella married Joe Baurerle.

Stepsons, Waldo, born 1902, March, married Nevada Davidson, parented four children, (1935) Jackie JoAnn, who is the mother of three, Jackie Wayne, Sherry and Randi Rockey; (1937); Hugh (Bud) who has one son, (1939) Waldo, Jr (Lou), who has three children, Allen, Lou Ann and Theresa; and (1947) Sue, who is the mother of two sons, Rick and Troy Green

Stepson, Ralph born 1904, March, married Helen Chesser, and they had one son, (1929-1932) William (Billy) (who died as a child) and one daughter, (1931-2010) Ida Barbara. He divorced and in 1947 married Mildred Hopkins. Mildred had a son who become part of the family and took on the Randall name, (1940-2005) Timothy Randall. Ralph and Mildred had also a son and a daughter, (1947) Gordon and (1952)

Rosemary. Barbara had two children, a son, Larry Lawdermilt, and a daughter. Tim had two sons. Gordon has one daughter, Lee, and Rosemary has three daughters, Corie, Abbie and Jill Edens.

Charles and Sarah's great-great-great grandchildren:

Wilbur's are listed in his section, The Wilbur Reynolds Family

Earnest Randall: (1) Shirley, born August 27, 1936, married Art Herzberg in 1954. Her children and grandchildren are: (Jesse Herzberg) born July 14, 1956, married Lynne and has Ann Marie (1978), Heather Ann (1979) and Christin (1981). Ann has three children, Dominick, Joselyn Rayann, and Kaylee; Heather has five children, Melina, Micah, Keona, Noelani and step son, Kobe. Christen has two children, Madison and Maeson.

(David Herzberg), born May 6, 1958, married Jan Williams, has two children, Brittany and Bradley.

(Mark Herzberg), born January 9, 1961, married Denise Mulryan, has Lisha Ann (1983) and Megan Marie and Tori Lynn.

(Valorie), born June 5, 1962, married Dave Sanders, has Kari Ann, (1982) and Matthew David. Kari is the mother of Samatha, and Matthew has Vincent and Zoe.

(2) Linda, born July 23, 1944, married James William (Bill) Martin in 1962. Her children and grandchildren are (Pamela), born May 13, 1964 and has Michael Keith Martin (1981).

(Melissa), born January 1, 1969, has daughter, Megan, who has a child.

(Michelle), born March 29, 1972, married to Jeff Cox, has two children, Kaitlin and Jared.

(3) Tom, born September 4, 1947, married Lee Manigiola in 1967. Their children are (Jason), born November 8, 1967, (Joshua), born November 30, 1971 and (Jennifer), born July 1, 1973.

Elizabeth Randall: (1) Charles William Robbins, (Bill) born April 23, 1937, married Rosalee Deloris Clarkson in 1957. Their children are (Charles Jeffery), born July 26, 1960, has Spencer (1987), Corbin (1991), and Conner (1994). Jeff is married to Jackie.

(Charlene Deloris,) born October 25, 1963 (deceased)

(Charla Kay), born May 12, 1965, married David Nash, has two daughters, Cassie (1991) and Victoria (1999). Charla and David are divorced.

(Cheryl), born August 4, 1966, married Rick Gibson, has two daughters, Allison (1994) and Michelle (1991). Cheryl and Rick are divorced.

(2) Donna Lou Robbins, born January 3, 1940 (died January 4, 1940)

(3) Karen Elizabeth Robbins, born July 31, 1943, married Donald Miles in 1962. Their son is (Donald Allen Miles), born August 30, 1963. Allen has five children, two girls and three boys. Karen was killed in 1965 by a drunken driver. Allen's children are Ashlyn Elizabeth, (1997), Loren (1999), Nicholas (Nick) (2003), Ryan (2005) and Logan (2007).

(4) Patricia (Patty), born June 7, 1948, married Dale Thompson in 1964 (divorced in 1979). They have two children, (Gregory Dale Thompson), born September 10, 1965, has a daughter, Kalissa (2004).

(Amy), born June 6, 1971, is married to Troy Lewis. They have one daughter, Kaitlyn, (1992).

Patty is married to Bill Robertson.

Stella Randall: (1)James Edward Fisher, born July 22, 1939, married Betty Walker. They adopted Timothy Lee Fisher and Angelia Lynn Fisher.

(2) Ida Belle Fisher, born August 3, 1941, married Harold Harding. They had one son, (Steven Harding), born December 19, 1960. Ida is married to Bud Mears.

(3).Robert Joe Fisher, born November 28, 1942, married Catherine Pyles in 1964. They had one son, (Jeffery Warren Fisher), born June 28, 1965, is married to Ginger and they have a daughter, Megan.

*I am also including Waldo and Ralph's family, because our grandmother made no distinction between her children and her stepsons, and we consider ourselves cousins, blood with standing.

Waldo Randall: (1)Jackie Joan, born May 17, 1935, married Robert (Bob) Rockey in 1955. Their children are (Jackie Wayne Rockey), born May 29, 1956, is married to Jean Ellis, have one son, Sean Aaron Rockey, ((1976), and two grandsons.

(Cheryl Ann Rockey), born April 17, 1961, is married to K. Edward Meek and they have two girls, Amanda (1980) and Rebecca (1983), and grandchildren.

(Randi Lee Rockey), born April 19, 1965, was married to Pickett, has two children, Justin and Savannah, and grandchildren.

(2) Hugh Francis Randall, born February 16, 1937, has son, (Mark Anthony), born March 14, 1975.

(3) Waldo Randall, Jr. (Lou), born September 25, 1939, married Charlotte Green in 1962, (Charlotte died in 1982). There are three children. (Lou Ann), born January 27, 1963, is married and has two children.

(Allen Randall), born January 10, 1964, and is married to Amy. They have two sons, Harrison and Ethan.

(Theresa Lynn), born April 3, 1968. She is married to Galmore.

Lou is married to Karel.

(4) Sue Lynn, born February 28, 1947, married Danny Green (who died in 2013) January 1, 1966. They had two sons, (Ricky Allen Green), born November 16, 1966, and (Troy Wayne Green), born July 6, 1972. Troy

and his wife, Christina, have three girls, Danielle, (1998), Hannah, (2002) and Phoebee, (2012). Ricky is married to Shelia and has three step-children, Lauren, Kaitlyn, & Evan.

Ralph Randall: (1) William Randall, (died as a very young child);

(2) Barbara Randall, born May 27, 1931, married a Lawdermilt, had a son (Larry Lawdermilt), born November 5, 1948. Larry has two daughters, Heather (1979) and Stephanie (1981).

Barbara married Virgil Woodson in1950 and had a daughter, (Linda Woodson), born September 6, 1951. Linda married Steven Overmire and has two children, Erika (1973) and Christopher (1976).

(3) Timothy Randall, born November 11, 1940, married Donna Baun and they had three sons, (Harvey Wayne), (died as a child), (Harvey Leon), born January 27, 1966 and (David Wade), born June 29, 1967. Timothy has grandchildren, Brandi, (1992), Courtney, (1997), Gabriel (1999) and Quinn Randall (2009), also Katrina, Ashley, Shannon, Jasmine, Jeremy and Justice. Timothy died in 2007.

(4) Gordon Randall, born August 14, 1947, married Jean Ann McCoy in 1972. They have one daughter, (Leigh), born October 29, 1973. Leigh is married to Cory Wilcoxson and has two daughters, Sidney (1998) and Molly (2000).

(5) Rosemary Randall, born January 15, 1952, married Dennis Edens in July of 1972. They have three daughters and three granddaughters. (Corrie), born April 17, 1973 is the mother of Sophia (1997).

(Abbie), born October 22, 1976.

(Jill), born March 23, 1978, is married to Jeff Stoner. She is the mother of Maggie (2008) and Emelia Mae (2012).

With this story I conclude the Zielger/Schneider portion of this ongoing saga.

It was Charles Ziegler's custom to send his grandson, Wilbur, to the nearby store to purchase for him a portion of pipe tobacco. (Unacceptable, of course, in today's society, but that was another time). SO on a particular day, Wilbur was sent to the store for tobacco, a task he enjoyed. But on this day, there was a new clerk, and he refused to sell the tobacco to the young child. When Dad returned and told his grandfather his story, Charles was livid. He marched my dad down to that store and pushed his way to the front of the line, and placing his hand on dad's shoulder, stuck his finger in that clerk's face, and declared loud enough for everyone in the store to hear. "You see this boy. He is my grandson, and when I send him for tobacco, you will sell him tobacco." No one in the store doubted that there would be no more problems with Wilbur bring home tobacco.

I believe when all is said and done, Charles Ziegler was an exceptional good man, but like my father he had a certain set of rules that were his alone, and God help the man who broke them.

Lord, Forgive

Lord, Forgive my whining;
It was just the timing!
It just hit me wrong.

But I wouldn't be minding
If I was busy binding
My heart to Yours!

So, Lord, help me with the climbing
And then I'll be finding,
Views that are out of this world!

Don't let me be pining
Or my teeth grinding.
Help me let the past and dead things go.

Help me be dining.
Upon your love lining
Every page of my days.

As you are defining
And refining
All that I am.

For in the ending
You are signing
The book of my life.

Arney-Foga History

So as Sarah Catherine married Charles Ziegler and became the Matriarch of our branch of family, so her cousin, Sophia, married Jacob Foga and became the Matriarch of a large, wide spreading family. This history included other family members, but Sophia seems to have given us the largest collection of Arney related cousins, whom we have enjoyed knowing and working with over the years. A special thanks to Lucy Foga Carpenter who is Sophia's daughter and has given me a lot of this history. It is she who came up to my mother one day at Regals and said to her, "my mother and your mother-in-law were first cousins."

Isaac Arney was born in Pennsylvania October 28, 1815 and died at Vernon August 12, 1888. He died of erysipelas, a very nasty disease that caused painful blisters especially in the mucous membranes. He appears to have come to Indiana as a single man. No other family connections can be found. Other Arney families settled on the western side of the state, but again no connections found. In Jennings County, he married Nancy Conner in 1844 and they had two little girls, Louisa (1848) and Charlotte (1851), and then Nancy died. I found no other mention of Louisa, but Aunt Charlotte married a Bush (I found her obituary) and died in Indianapolis. It was in 1857 that Isaac married Diantha Davis who also had a child, a son, Lewis Bryan. (He is buried next to Isaac and Diantha at the cemetery in Vernon). He was a Civil War veteran. It appears he never married. Also Nathan or Nathaniel is buried there and shares a stone with his parents. He died seven days after his father, but of an ear disease. (?) He was only 24 years old but was married. AS far as we can determine, Isaac worked for other farmers, never had land of his own. The area they lived in was in Vernon township somewhere in the vicinity of Goose or Crooked Creeks. Charles and Sarah may have met at the Ebenezer Methodist Church which was nearby.

Isaac and Diantha's other children are as follows: They had twelve children all together, nine were born to the two of them.

And that first child of their own was our great grandmother, Sarah Catherine Arney, born April 10, 1859. Her family is listed in the preceding section.

(2) Charles Arney, born 1861, died in Oklahoma, married to Sadie

(3) Nathan, born 1864, died 1888, in Vernon.

(4) Mary Elizabeth Arney, born 1862, married William Gribble in 1884.

(5) Willaim O. Arney, born 1866, married Noretta Oldham in 1891. Died in1934.

(Edia May), or (Edna) born July 1892 m. Leeds, 3 children, Rose, Bobby, & Floyd.

(Sophia), born April 1896, m. Jacob Foga (more following section)

(Grace B.), born Feb 1899, died as a baby

(Goldie) m. John Blavett, children are Margie, Freida, Doris, Frankie & Harry.

(Iva) m. Carl Pool, 9 children. (lived in Florida) Carl, Hope, Iris, Billy, David, Velma and Sondra.

(Clara), married Russell Flint, and later an Eden, died in 1998. Children are Rowina, Miles, Gene, Cecil, Homer, and Jeraldine.

(Walter), married Margaret Day. Children are Dorothy, Betty, Helen, Teresa, Janis, & John (Columbus area).

(6) Isaac, Jr. (Smith), born 1869, m. Cora McCoy in 1890. Died in 1940.

(Roy), born July 21, 1891, married to Rosa, sons Wm, Tom, Paul and Robert.

(Cecil), born August 7, 1895

(Bertha), born 1899, died 1901.

(Ulysess Howard) (Curly), born March 25, 1909. His mother died in 1910. Our great grandmother, Sarah, took the young family in and helped raise the family, especially Howard. Our father and he were raised more like brothers and were always close. Howard ran a garage in Vernon for many years. Howard was married to Golda Myrick and had two sons and two daughters. They are Ken who lived in Vernon and I visited. His son, Richard, died in 1993 in an automobile accident. There was also Cecil who lives in Louisana and Marilyn who married Floyd Tungeitt. She has descendents in the area. There was also a Betty who married an Evans.

(7) Bertha (Birdie), born 1872, married James MCQuitha in 1890. (Jim), whose children were Jim and Ruth and (Wilma) who married Mike Kirchner and children are Nancy, Jake and Dennis.

(8) Samuel, born 1875, married Julia Marlett in 1893. (John), (Mary), (William) and (Pearl) who married Lou Speer and had six children, Andy, Leo, Lula (m Henry Seger), Julia (m Thomas Kane), Nancy (m Morris and later Charles Vogel) and Mary (m Fred Biehle). The Biehles' children (some of them) live locally. They are Edna (m Egan), Freda Ann (m Henry), Amy, Leona (m Senbers), Andrew, Bill and Katy (who married Roy Matthews, who grew up in our neighborhood around Brewersville). Roy and Katy have all girls whom I have met briefly.

Two additional notes on Samuel's family. Lula and Julia were the ages of Aunt Elizabeth and Aunt Stella, and went to school with them at Vernon. During those school years, Lula and Julia often came out to the farm and spent the night.

Fred Biehle, who married Mary Arney, knew my dad when Fred was a boy. Our dad worked for Fred's family and planned to marry Fred's sister, but she died.

More Foga Family

Remember William's daughter, Sophia Arney, married Jacob Foga. She had eight children. Many stayed in this area. These are their families.

(Lucy) married Arthur Carpenter. Her children are Daniel, Ronnie, Donna (whose children include Tracey), Carol who married Rick Ketcham and Barbara who married Jim Prewitt (whose children include Heather and Jason).

(Franklin) married JoAnn Mullis. Their children are Dale, Lois, Jacob and Rita. I have met the daughters.

(Henry) married Betty Harp. Their children are Charles, (whom I went to school with), Carol, Janis, Larry, Tom, Gloria and Anna. I have met Tom's sons, Henry and William or Willie who went to school with my Daniel. I worked with Larry's wife, Mary, and they have a son, Eric who has children.

(George) married Margaret Harp. Their children are Karen who is married to a Kasper and they have two sons. Linda who married Billy Mullikin and has two daughters, Kelli and? and a son and grandchildren. There is also Terry and Carla who have two children a piece. I worked with Karen and have met Linda and one of her daughters.

(John) had five children, Jana, Kevin, Kent, Nancy and Dennis

(William Louis) died as a child.

(Leo) married, had three children, Jerry, Sharon and Danny.

(Bernice) married Charles Clark. She had no children.

*At the time of this writing,(2014), Lucy is the only one of her siblings living as the only one living in our family is Aunt Stella who just turned 96. Remember their grandparents were brother and sister.

There are many, many other Foga and Arney descendents not listed since I got this list, but I simply could not get all the information gathered together. Following is the Foga Family Reunion write up from the Jennings County paper in 1998 and since then they continue to grow, just as our family does. But this simply shows, there are cousins, cousins, cousins everywhere.

Foga Reunion

Foga family reunion, a total of 68 people, enjoyed home cooking, games and visiting. Attending were Tim, Rita, Brianna and Dorianna Horn, Lois Smith, Trent, Trevor, Trena and Seairra FOga. Lucy Carpenter; Barb, Heather and Jason Prewitt; Linda and Bill Mullikin; Kelli Mullikin and Adrianne Garris; Jean and Cindy Hammond; Henery and Betty Foga; Brenda, Robert, Bobbi and Shawn Green; Marcy, Brandi, Melinda and Allison Turner; and Jacob, Linda and Sean Foga. Also, Tom, Dee, Nona, Michelle, and William Foga; Henry, Leann and Aaron Foga; Terry, Liz and Killy Foga: Karen Kasper; Dale, Donna, Josh, and Pam Hayes; Terry and Anna Fletcher and family; Lisa and Caleb Hayes; Dean and Mary Fletcher & family; Marie Foga; Charlie Foga; Danny O& Sue Carpenter; Scott Black and family; Carol, Alex and Alyssa Hill; Sherry Fulton; Ron & Joye Carpenter & family; Larry, Mary, & Eric Foga; and Paul, Carla, Michael and Amber Sharp.

Announcements for last year. Anna Foga James and Terry Fletcher were married May of 1997.
Rita Fog Horn and Tim Horn had a daughter, Dorianna Renae, born July 2, 1997.
Jeremy and Lisa Hayes had a son, Caleb Allen, born September 17, 1997.
1998: Carol Fletcher Hall and Scott Hill had a daughter, Alyssa Jane, born Feb 4.
Kelli Sue Mullikin and T. J. Garris had a daughter, Adrianne Irene, born March 31.
Trena Foga had a daughter, born June 4.
Shannon Hammond Holwager and Bob Holwager had a son, Dylan Michael, born April 7.
Brett Carpenter and Angie Nestor were married June 27.

Josh Sharp and Heather Mullins were married in May.

This concludes the Foga/ Arney History, but I am adding a fictional sketch, called, "The First Diantha".

The First Diantha in America

She stood on the deck, oblivious to the salt water spray that dampened her hair and clothes. She faced westward, but her heart looked the other way. Yesterday was behind her and tomorrow in front of her but today was cold and leaden. She was going to America. For many, that was a long sought dream, but not for her. She was going because she felt she had no other choice. She turned and took one long look at the shoreline and then bowed her head. She would never see Ireland again. Her parents were dead, her brother in prison and her sisters with too little for their own growing families. Her brother had urged her to do this, offer herself as an indentured servant, and thusly get ship passage to America. He assured her after she got settled with a family, he would come too. It would have helped so much if she did not have to do this alone.

The spray was turning her curly red hair even curlier. It was the color of her father's. Oh, how she missed him. He had a way with the fiddle and a way with words, and he had loved his family and he had loved Ireland. She could still hear his voice in her memory and could remember how her mother would give him loving little pats, as she went about her work in the small cottage.

As she sadly turned away from the rail, she clutched her shawl closer. It had been made by her mother and she hoped she did not lose it. It was the only tangible thing she possessed that her mother's hands had touched, made from their own wool, too. She was going to try to keep alive in her heart the hope of better days. She would first hope for a kind family to take her indenture and then she would hope that they be Irish, or Scottish or even English. It would be more like home if they weren't German or Dutch.

Loralyn Reynolds

The sea was getting choppy so she needed to go below, but she dreaded it. The ship was small, overcrowded, and smelly. And it would get smellier before the six to eight weeks passed that would bring them to American shores. It would smell of vomit and sweat and unwashed bodies and sickness and death. She knew she was healthy but she may be skin and bones before this voyage was complete. Ship's food was sometimes not even tolerable. The ship lurched and she stumbled toward the stairs which could better be described as a hanging ladder. She slowly made her way down into the darkness, the interior darkness pierced only by a little light coming from the hatch and a couple oil lamps. Finally, she looked around her and really looked at those she traveled with. Some would become friends. Some would have to be watched carefully because they would steal and some men would have to be avoided. And some, friend or foe, would die. None of these ships ever arrived without a number of deaths. She shuddered. Hope, it was hope she must keep alive, in herself and she must be contagious with this hope, for no one could need it more than the wretched looking group she saw before her. She must try to be like the flickering light and remember that to push back the darkness, one must light a lamp and remember the source of her spiritual oil, in God alone.

HN: I do not know if the first Diantha was an indentured servant but I am sure there were at least one somewhere in our family history. The name Diantha or Dicey or Dicey Ann, all names referring to our own ancestor, was used often in the Davis family, so I am relatively sure it was used before the name was given to our great-great grandmother. And I am so grateful for those ancestors who braved those choppy seas and stinky little boats to secure for their descendents a better life. Some made it and some did not.

GENERATION CHART FOR Nora DETAMORE

Siblings*
William 1923*
Wendell 1924*   Link Coan+
Phillip 1928*   (first husband)

Siblings+
Highley 1912+
Lillian 1917+
Mary Ann1919+
Martha1 921+

Percy O. Detamore*
July 18, 1899-1981
m. Apr 23, 1923

Madge Highley
Oct 2, 1889-1976

Nora Detamore *
B: Jan 7, 1927
m. Feb 24, 1947

(Husband)Wilbur Reynolds

Deloss Detamore   Leroy Highley
Nov 8, 1869-1938   Jan 31, 1844-1927
m.Sep 5, 1891   m. Jan 27, 1889

Nora Rust   Ida Culp
Feb 10, 1873-1915   Oct 30, 1866-1950

Eli Detamore   John Rust   Clark Highley   Lewis Culp
Nov 7,1848-1914   1825-1908   Oct 1815-1888   Nov 12,1836-1914
m. Aug 30, 1866   m.   m.   m. Nov 14, 1863

Mary Snyder   Eliza   Telitha   Harriet McBee
Apr 23, 1844-1910   Aug 4,1820-1893   May 5, 1839-1918

William Detamore   John Culp
May 21,1807-1888
m. Apr 15, 1826   m.   m.
Margaret Shulll   Mary Bechtol
1807-1863

Samuel McBee
m.
Jane H.

Nora's great-great-great grandparents that we know of include Jacob Detamore (VA) and Sophia Lenks, who was born July 14, 1783, exactly 200 years before her ggggg grandson, Daniel Melvin. Margaret Shull's parents were Jacob and Elizabeth Hinsel Shull. Jacob Detamore's father, Jacob Christian (1755) Detamore, was a Hessian soldier who stayed in Virginia. He married Elizabeth Coaler, daughter of Henry Coaler. The Detamores, Highleys, Culps, Bechtols and McBees were all from Virginia, the latter three families were in West Virginia after 1863, and Lewis fought on the northern side in the Civil War as did Leroy Highley, John Rust, and Eli Detamore. John Rust was born in Ohio and died in Indiana.

Percy Detamore

Debas Detamore & sons

Nora Rust & sister

Percy, Bud & Bob

His Brothers and sisters
Fern, Roy, Dunc, Mary, Ivan, Percy
Forrest, Viola (Bud), Cecil (Pete)

Dunc & family

Danny & Verdyn, Mike Fort →
Forr Danny →

Merle Ross' family

Fern, Roy, Dunc, Ivan & Pete

The Detamores or Detamore/
Reynolds or Reynolds/Detamore

This book is mainly about our family but it is also about Jennings County. As already stated, my dad's people have been in Jennnings County for nearly two hundred years. My Mom's folks have been here nearly one hundred years. In the local thinking, Mom's folks are newcomers. I'm not going to spend a lot of time on this section for two reasons, one is Mom's family has been touched on in the first section, and two, her family history needs more research. It has been easier to work on Dad's side of the family, since the focus was Jennings County.

So here I go to share with you what I do know.

One thing I know, the spelling may have changed. Chances are the early ancestors did not know how to spell their names, so they spoke the name and census takers and other officials took a guess at spelling it. In the 1810 Virginia census, three Detamore brothers, names spelled slightly different, Determon, Detimon and Detimore. In the 1830 census, our ancestor, William, spelling Detamore, brothers Henry, Detmore, brother Jacob, Detmore, and brother, George, Dettamon. Other possible spellings are too numerous to recount but here are some examples are Detmer, Dediemar, Dettmer, Detmor, Dittimore, Ditmore. Even in my mother's generation, she says her maiden name differently than does her brothers.

And to let you know, there are three books on Detamore history. I have copies of all. They don't agree in many spots. I trust the first and third one more readily, and the newer one is updated to my mother's generation and to mine.

In 1915, my great-grandfather, Deloss Detamore, brought his family to Jennings County. They lived on a farm where the house sets on a hill near Graham Church. His wife, Nora Rust, had died that year giving birth to their fourteenth child, Robert (Bob). They had been living near Converse. I do not know why he chose Jennings County.

According to the "100 Years Ago", a well read section of the local paper, there were many families that seemed to move regularly between (Marion) Grant County and Jennnings. One reason may have been the glass factory that operated in Jennings County and was first staffed by Grant County men of experience. Regardless, Deloss didn't stay long in Jennings, maybe four years. In that time, two young daughters fell in love or something with two local boys, and so they stayed to become the nucleus of what I would come to refer to as the Jennings County Aunts. One was Ivan, born in 1900, who married George Graham and lived on Graham Creek and had five children, Glen, Doris, Georgiana, John and Katherine (Kate). The other was (Dona) or May Ora, born 1905, who married Jim Hoffman and raised her four children at Lovett, Daisy, Mary Lou, James (Elmer) and Dean. Dean's birth, May 3, 1945 is significant for this reason.

On May 2, 1945, my grandfather, Percy Odwic Detamore brought his household goods, animals and two youngest children, Phillip (Raggs) and Nora to Jennings County. He had bought a little farm in western Lovett Township and was planning on going back to farming. His two oldest sons were serving in Europe and the war to end all wars was not yet over. They had planned to spend the night with Dona before unloading and settling in at the farm. And that is what they did, but early the next morning, Dr. John Green had to be called and he routed everyone with loud loquacity, words I will not repeat here, but be sure, he wanted everyone out of the house who would not prove useful to helping him bring a baby boy into the world. So, my grandfather, Mick, and Mom and Uncle Raggs went to the farm while back in Lovett, Dean Hoffman was born. Dean was a child of midlife and more my age than my mother's to whom he is a first cousin. Aunt Dona said he was the joy of her life, and I am sure that was true. His nephew, Allen Cunningham, is only a year younger. Allen is the son of Mary Lou and John Cunningham. Dona's other grandchildren were Daisy's three sons, Richard (Dick), Paul and David. Daisy was married to Dick Jordan, who helped Grandpa bring stuff from Marion. Other grandchildren are Dean's two sons, Travis and Dustin, for Elmer never married. Great grandchildren include Allen's two daughters and Paul's daughter and son and Richard and Nellerene's two sons and a daughter. I believe David has two sons.

Back to the farm. Nora and Raggs weren't as excited about the farm as Grandpa but made an attempt. Raggs found he was doing most of the work and that got old quick. For Nora, there were not enough boyfriends, only two. One became my father. Interestingly both were willing or I should say both wanted to marry my mother. She and Uncle Raggs did go back to Marion for awhile in 1946. Mom worked in a shoe factory for awhile and stayed with Uncle Bill and his new wife, Eunice. Uncle Raggs decided the army was preferable to the farm and joined and was sent to Europe right away. Mom then came back to Jennings County and married my dad, Wilbur Reynolds in February of 1947. They lived with Grandpa for several months. To help with my birth and because she, too, wanted to experiment with country life, my great Aunt Pete bought a farm near my grandfather's in Lovett Township. She brought with her from Marion not only household goods but her daughter and son-in-law and three grandchildren. During the war, she had lost her only son, James. She became the third Jennings County aunt, and the one I spent the most time with. She asked in return for caring for me and my mother after my birth that she be allowed to name me and she did, the name Lora Lyn, a name that my mother, Nora, could easily spell and went with all the other family names, her daughter, Lenora and her granddaughter, Doralee. Her other grandchildren were boys, James (Jim), Charles and Tom. We spent most holidays with this family and the older children were always very protective and watchful of Danny and me. Only Tom was younger. Tom has two daughters. Charles has one son. Jim has a daughter and Doralee had two sons and a daughter. Aunt Pete, born in 1895, lived to be 99 years old.

Our great Aunt Mary, born 1901, was the Marion or Grant County Aunt. She married Ed Stephenson and was the mother of fourteen children, nine raised to adulthood. They are John, Ruby, Jack, Joseph (Joe Dan), Walter Leroy, the twins, Leona and Lenora, Larry and Nora Marlene. Aunt Mary and her kids here and there would come visit us in Jennings County. Aunt Mary loved flowers, and I remember when she dug up some redbud from our woods and took them back to plant in her Gas City home. I have a list of her grandchildren and great-grandchildren.

The Indianapolis aunt was Aunt Fern, born 1911. She married George Hedges and had only two children, Gerald (who died as a child from rabies) and Judith Ann (Judy). Judy is married to Pete Fischer.

The other aunt is one I never met. She died when only thirty. Aunt Tressie, born 1896, did marry and had three children, Robert (Bob) Bennett and Leona Bennett and Harold (died in infancy). Bob had three sons, David, Wayne and Larry. I had dinner with and visited with David and Wayne and their wives when I worked in New Castle. I had not seen them since they were children and they last attended a Detamore reunion. Leona married Irwin Wyne and had two children, Raymond and Nora (m. Wagers). Leona has two grandchildren. I got to meet David's daughter and grandchildren, also. They also had a daughter that they lost in her teens. Wayne had three children and Larry two.

My great uncles were all Grant County uncles. There was Roy, born 1910 and Bob, born 1915. (I dearly loved them) and Forrest (Fats), born 1892 and Volney, (Bud), born 1893, Detamore. I do not remember Uncle Bud or Uncle Fats. They both died in 1952 and I was only five years old. Uncle Bud never married and Forrest, who married Rose, had three sons, two never married. His son, Harry made up for his brothers by having eight children. I only remember meeting David who came to reunion several times. He had two sons.

Uncle Bob had one daughter, Beatrice (Pooch) and two granddaughters. His wife was also Beatrice or Aunt Bea.

Uncle Roy had three sons, Rollin (Butch), Paul and Kirk. There are eight grandchildren. He was married to Marie and they lived on Ninth Street as did Uncle Bob.

Deloss and Nora had three children, Dorothy, John, and Russell who died as children.
*I have the names of many of the grandchildren and great greats, thanks to Judy Fischer, who compiled and updated the Detamore History. It just didn't seem to be a part of this particular book. If interested I can

copy Judy's pages for you or the original history, which is summed up as follows.

Jacob Detamore was born in Hesse Cassel, Germany about 1750 and subject to the military laws of the Hesse province, governed by a Duke. In 1776, during the War of Revolution, the English government hired 17,000 troops from the Duke. The troops were shipped to America under the command of Lord Howe and arrived in July of 1776. Jacob Detamore was one of that number. Part of the troops were placed under General Cornwallis.

It is not known whether our ancestor was with the troops that surrendered in 1977 or with the troops that surrendered to Washington in 1781 at Yorktown. The tradition is that five years after landing in America, our Jacob passed through picket lines and finished out the war with the colonial forces. Which ever story is true, it is known that he was a Hessian soldier fighting as a mercenary in the service of King George of England. After the war, he chose to remain in America, married and settled in Rockingham County, Virginia (Shenandoah Valley) He became a minister in the German Reformed church. He was held in high esteem by neighbors and friends and was referred to as Old Granddad Detamore. He and his wife were parents of six children.

OF their six children, our direct ancestor is another Jacob (wife Sophia Lenks) and through his son William, (wife Margaret Shull) who is the father of Eli who is the father of Deloss. Eli was actually born in Ohio and fought in the Civil War. Eli's wife was Mary Snyder. The family slowly migrated westward, and Grandpa was born in Howard County, Indiana in 1899, the fifth child and third son of Deloss and Nora Rust Detamore.

Our grandfather, Percy Odwic Detamore, was born July 18, 1899 and died in 1981. He married my grandmother, Madge Bell Highly in April of 1943. She already had four children and should never have had any. Her children by A.L. Coan were Highly, Lillian, Mary Ann and Martha Coan. The four children Madge and Mick had together were William (Bill), Wendell (Lefty), Nora, and Phillip (Raggs). As far as geography goes, Martha and Lillian ended up in California; Mary

Ann in Michigan and Mom in Jennings County. All the boys stayed in Marion.

(1) Highly had two daughters and a son, Dick, Barbara, and Betty. Uncle Hi died when I was still in my teens. He was born in 1911 or 1912.

(2) Lillian, born 1917, much later in life, adopted two children

(3) Mary Ann, born in 1919, married Will Decker. She lost a child and could not have any more. Will told her he loved her but wanted children, so he divorced her. She said if I can't have the man I want, I don't want a man and she never remarried.

(4) Martha, born January of 1921, married the father of her sons, Art Jones. Her children were Michael and Art. Michael was killed in his early twenties. We have lost track of Art. Martha was married to a Moore at the time of her death. We visited these California aunts on our way to Washington State when Charles was on The Fox.

(5) Bill, born William Allen Detamore, on June 27, 1923 in Ohio. He married Eunice McCarty in February of 1946. They had three children, Billie, born December 26, 1946, Rebecca, born August 25, 1949, and Jackie Lee, born June 25, 1952. Billie has four children, and Becky and Jackie each have one.

(6) Lefty, born Wendell Odwic Detamore on June 22, 1924, in Ohio. He married the Buck Town girl who had always loved him, Mary Ethel Renn in 1943. They had five children, Wendell Allen, (Buster) born in 1944, Berniece, born November 1, 1946, Marilyn Sue, born June 9, 1952, and Rick, born sometime. A fifth child died in infancy. Buster has three sons; Niecey, a son and a daughter; Marilyn, a daughter and two sons, and Rick, also two sons and a daughter.

(7) Nora Elizabeth Detamore, born January 7, 1927 in Butler, Ohio. She married Wilbur Reynolds in 1947 and had two children. Loralyn, born April 20, 1947 and Danny Warren, born October 1, 1948. Loralyn has three children and Danny has two daughters.

(8) Raggs, born Phillip Warren Detamore, on November 28, 1928, in Converse, Indiana, died in December of 2002. He married Betty Betts in January of 1953. They had two daughters, Debra, born November 30, 1953 and Phyllis, born, August 1, 1956. Debbie has a son and Phyllis two daughters.

All three of Mick Detamore's sons served in the Armed Forces. They all came home, and raised families.

*The Detamore reunion is still held the third Sunday of August in Marion or nearby and has been held over a hundred years.

My grandfather's mother, Nora Rust, was born in 1873. Her father was John Rust, born in Ohio. She had two sisters, Angie and Jane. One married a Detamore. John Rust fought in the Civil War, was about 5 foot, 5 inches according to my grandfather. I have a picture of him with his second wife, Anna. Grandpa said he thought his grandmother's name was Eliza.

My mother's mother was a Highley, the daughter of Leroy Highley. She had a half sister, Anna. Her other siblings were Lula (m Witt, one son); Clova, (m Chester Endsley, no children); Harriet (married Paul Spencer, four sons); Edna (m Wesley Crandall, had one son and four daughters); McKinley (married Thelma, one son) (married Helen, had five children); Mark (married Willa, had two sons and two daughters).

Leroy Highley's parents were Clark and Telitha Highley. He had six siblings, Anslem, Daniel, James, William, Mary Ann and Liona. Leroy was a Civil War veteran, was with Sherman in the Carolina campaign. Leroy was a gentlemen farmer and taught school.

The Highley's had a land grant that indicated they were in Indiana by 1849 but I think Leroy was born in Indiana so they were here before

1844. They came from Virginia. I haven't researched it but I think the Highley farm was in northern Grant County on the Grant/Miami County line.

My mother's mother's mother was Ida Culp and she was born in Morgan County, West Virginia during the Civil War. She and her brother, Tom, came west to work, presumably for the Highley's. Their parents were Lewis Culp and Harriet McBee and Lewis, too was a Civil war Veteran, drew a pension. I have some of his military papers.

Ida's siblings were Tom, John (grandfather to our Pensacola cousin, John Culp), George, James, Emma, Samuel and William.

Harriet's parents were Samuel and Jane McBee. Jane did weaving. Harriet had the following siblings: Emaline, Sarah, Alice, Lucinda, James and Catherine per 1860 census. She easily could have had older siblings. There was a Joseph McBee, age 25, working for a physician and living in his household. This could have been a brother. 1880 census indicates a sister named Mary, the age of sister, Sarah or this could have been Emaline whose middle name started with M. Census takers were not always too careful with their documentation.

In that same 1860 census, Lewis is listed with his birth family. He was the son of John Culp and Mary Bechtol. Siblings were Susan, older, and younger siblings, Catherine, Elizabeth, George, Henry, E (Female) name unreadable and male, Jer, also John B and F.H., female. Lewis was 21 at the time. His mother, Mary had a brother named Aaron and a brother named Lewis. All gave Virginia as place of birth.

The John Culp mentioned above is a cousin I met while we were assigned in Pensacola. I was working on family history and called two John Culps that were in the phone book. One never answered. The other was flabbergasted. I told him who I was and what I knew and asked if he was related. He didn't know. He didn't plan on calling me again, but curiosity got the best of him, and he called his dad, and found out that he was related. His dad remembered both his Aunt Ida and Uncle Tom who had gone to Indiana. So John called me back. We invited him and his wife for dinner and it was the beginning of a wonderful friendship.

And that is the most rewarding part of doing family research, finding cousins and connections that enrich our lives. An older cousin once told me I would someday find a cousin that I would regret finding, but so far I have not. Are you my cousin?????

I like adding a couple recipes to my books, especially something mentioned in the stories.

Shredded Wheat Rolls (Rolls to Die For)

2 biscuits of shredded wheat or mixture of ½ cup shredded wheat, ½ cup oats, and 2 T. wheat germ.
3 T margarine and 3 T of brown sugar
1/3 cup each of oil and honey
1 and 1/2 teas salt

Place the above in a heavy mixing bowl
Pour 2 cups boiling water over the contents. When lukewarm, sprinkle 2 packages of yeast over mixture. Stir in. Throw dish towel over bowl and let set a few minutes (up to an hour). Then stir in 2 cups whole wheat flour and gradually add up to 3 cups white flour to make soft dough. Knead briefly. Place in greased bowl and grease top. Let rise until double and then make rolls or cover with plastic wrap and place in refrigerator up to three days and make rolls as needed.

When making rolls, let rise until double or to size desired. Bake at 375 or 400 degrees, 8-10 minutes. ({This recipe came from the Columbus newspaper in the 1970s. I believe Ralph, my step dad, gave it to me and I adapted it.llr)

Crescent rolls

Scald ¾ cup milk. Add 5 T margarine, 6 T sugar and 1 ½ teas salt. Cool to lukewarm. Sprinkle 2 pkgs. Dry yeast over ½ cup warm water. Stir to dissolve. Stir in the lukewarm milk mixture. Beat one egg and add. Add 2 cups flour. Beat until smooth. Stir in gradually 2 to 2 ½ cups of flour until a soft dough has formed. Knead until smooth and elastic. Place in greased bowl and cover. Keep in refrigerator two hours up to three days or let rise until double and punch down to make rolls. Make rolls. Let rise until double. Bake at 400 degrees until brown. Rolls are made by dividing dough into three sections. Roll each section into 8 inch round. Spread with soft margarine. Cut into 8 pie shaped wedges. Roll from large side to make crescent shape.

(These rolls were a 4H recipe and at age 14 Aunt Elizabeth showed me how to make them and then I taught Jean. (llr)

Turkey Noodle Soup

After taking most of turkey off the bones, store meaty bones until ready to make soup, refrigerator for three days or freezer. When ready to make soup, put meaty bones in large pan. Add one or two potatoes, washed with skins, a carrot, peeled, a piece of celery and a large onion, and salt and pepper to taste. Cook for about 30 minutes after it comes to a boil or until vegetables are tender and meat is falling off the bones. Remove meat, and vegetables, and bones. Discard bones after making sure all meat is pulled off. Set veggies aside. Bring broth to a rolling boil (May have to add some canned broth or I use a chicken bouillon cube to a cup of water). Add homemade noodles. Stir well and reduce heat. Cook until noodles are desired doneness. The add back veggies after chopping them some; also, add meat. May add more leftover turkey as desired. I prefer very little meat. Very good served with whole wheat rolls.

Turkey or Chicken Casserole

Mix together 4 cups chopped cooked turkey or chicken, 2 cups chopped celery, ¼ cup chopped onion, 2 cups croutons and 6 oz of shredded Swiss or provolone cheese. Mix together 1 cup miracle whip and ½ cup milk and add to the meat mixture. Top with almonds. Put into greased baking dish and bake in 350 degree oven for 35 minutes.

Chicken or Turkey Salad

If using leftover Holiday turkey, skip directions for cooking chicken. If using chicken, place 2 and ½ pounds of chicken breast in crock pot with a little salt and pepper and onion salt or dried onion and cook until tender. Shred meat and add cereal bowl of chopped celery and as many red grapes. Put in half a jar of salad dressing or until moistened to desired consistency. Then add chopped pecans. (Danny Reynolds)